A story of
motherhood by

_____

REALISTIC

SELF
CARE
for
Moms

REALISTIC

SELF
CARE
for
Moms

A Guided Journal for Taking Care
of *You* While Taking Care of Them

ABIGAIL DOSEN

Publisher: Peg Couch
Book Designer: Llara Pazdan
Editor: Colleen Dorsey
Art credits at bottom right

Library of Congress Control Number: 2024948552

ISBN: 978-0-7643-6950-6
Printed in China
10 9 8 7 6 5 4 3 2 1

Published by Better Day Books, an imprint of Schiffer Publishing, Ltd.

BETTER DAY BOOKS®

Better Day Books
Email: hello@betterdaybooks.com
Web: www.betterdaybooks.com
Visit us on Instagram!
@better_day_books

Schiffer Publishing
4880 Lower Valley Road
Atglen, PA 19310
Phone: 610-593-1777
Fax: 610-593-2002
Email: info@schifferbooks.com
Web: www.schifferbooks.com

For our complete selection of fine books on this and related subjects, please visit our website at www.betterdaybooks.com. You may also write for a free catalog.

Better Day Books titles are available at special discounts for bulk purchases for sales promotions or premiums. Special editions, including personalized covers, corporate imprints, and excerpts, can be created in large quantities for special needs. For more information, contact the publisher.

Dedication

To my children, you have each profoundly changed my
life in such a wonderful way, and I am honored to be
your mom. And to my husband, for showing me limitless
support, encouragement, and love. I cherish the beautiful
life we have created together.

Contents

Preface 8

Introduction 10

How to Use This Book 12

Chapter 1: Self-Love 23
Unpacking self-care and mom guilt

Chapter 2: Nourishment 37
Embracing mealtimes as a source of fuel and loving kindness

Chapter 3: Mindful Rest 49
Prioritizing adequate rest with intentional habits

Chapter 4: Personal Appearance 61
Embracing the layers of our outward presence with pride

Chapter 5: Quiet Time 75
The quest to find quiet in the midst of chaos

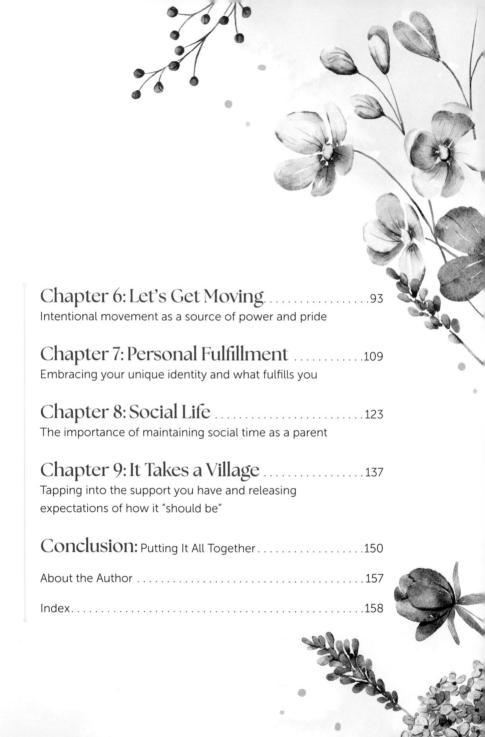

Chapter 6: Let's Get Moving 93
Intentional movement as a source of power and pride

Chapter 7: Personal Fulfillment 109
Embracing your unique identity and what fulfills you

Chapter 8: Social Life 123
The importance of maintaining social time as a parent

Chapter 9: It Takes a Village 137
Tapping into the support you have and releasing
expectations of how it "should be"

Conclusion: Putting It All Together 150

About the Author 157

Index 158

Preface

Hi there, I'm Abby. First of all, I'm so thankful that you decided to pick up my book. Writing this book has been a labor of love and tenderness. I have learned and grown along the way while writing it, and I hope that you will find my words to be meaningful in your path to self-love and self-discovery. I appreciate your time and energy, and I know that your dedication to growth will leave you feeling like a new person by the end of our journey together.

I've heard it said many times over that at the moment a child is born, a mother is born too. From the first second you lay eyes on your new baby, a fundamental shift in you as a human being has begun. Throughout your journey together, your precious child will experience their life with you as their guide and teacher. They will grow physically and emotionally every day with you by their side. What a phenomenal gift. What a dream come true. What an utterly incredible responsibility. Oh, and just a little bit of pressure, right?

There are countless resources out there for how to raise a baby, but where are all the guides on how to raise a mother? Specifically, how to be a fulfilled individual who takes care of and nurtures her unique self while also taking care of and nurturing her family?

As a mother to three little girls, I've grappled with this for four years and counting. I've searched high and low; I've read articles, books, and journals, listened to podcasts, and scrolled on social media. Yet still I experienced an unending feeling of being a little on my own in my journey toward becoming a calm, confident, and capable mom. I was desperately craving some sort of map to convince myself that I was on the right track, a resource to prove to me that becoming a mother, as fundamentally life-altering as it is, doesn't mean that I, as a person, am completely lost to the needs of my children. I was looking for a guide to remind me that as an individual, I still have value and worth. As I talked with more and more mothers, I realized that many of these women felt the same way.

I was searching for a guided journal to help me incorporate self-care into my daily life so I could avoid three things:

1. burning out completely from the tedious tasks involved in mothering;

2. growing the seeds of resentment as I watched friends and family move forward in careers, endeavors, and passions while I was "stuck" in my mom era; and

3. missing out on the opportunity for gratitude and appreciation for all of the good moments in the day-to-day of being a mom *because* of numbers 1 and 2!

The bad news is, I couldn't find such a journal.

The good news is, I wrote it!

Of course, I didn't just sit down one day and create this book in one easy, fell swoop. It took guts and a lot of hard work. I had had an inclination to become an author for much of my adult life, but I never really thought I would achieve it. After becoming a mom, I said to myself countless times that I would never be an author because I was "just" a mom. I had aspired to be a mom for so long, but that came with the weight of feeling like I didn't understand who I was outside of motherhood. It wasn't until after I started taking ownership of my needs and goals and learning to silence my impostor syndrome that I was able to clear the path and embrace my role as an author—as well as embracing all the other unique and beautiful elements that make me me. I was able to divert myself from the path of the tired, resentful mother who finds herself entirely engulfed in motherhood.

This passion project, this reflective journal, helped me find who *I* am while I was writing it to help you find who *you* are and who *you* want to be in this wild and beautiful journey of life. I'm so glad you're here.

Introduction

Stop what you're doing now and check the date on the calendar. Happy re-birthday, mama! Today is the day that you embark on a journey of self-discovery and self-love. You are about to be reborn as a mother who loves and cares for herself too. And I have the privilege and pleasure of being your guide on this messy, lifelong trek of life after birth.

If you had asked me throughout my life what I wanted to be when I grew up, the answer always included being a mother. I chose teaching as a career because it felt as close to mothering as I could get within a job, and I dreamed of the day that I would have my own baby to cherish and love. When this dream was fulfilled and my first daughter was born, I soon began to understand that I was entirely unaware of what being a mother truly meant. Of course, there was all the joy and love that I had expected, but I had underestimated the limitless logistical and practical tasks associated with taking care of another human being. I had also underestimated the enormous transformation that would occur in me.

There is so much more to being a mom than simply raising your children. You're also responsible for growing your own self and uncovering who you are as a person in an entirely different way. The stakes feel high because the stakes *are* high: your child or children look to you as an example, and as mothers we need to set our own intentional and authentic example through the way we live.

Over the four years that I have been a mother, I have constantly strived to be a good parent while also accepting and embracing the truth that I, too, deserve to flourish in personal ways outside of mothering. Acknowledging this has helped me find fulfillment, contentment, and joy despite the many demands of life as a parent. And you deserve this too! That is what this book is for and why I wrote it.

My deepest hope as you read and reflect on the words in these chapters is that you, too, can find the intersection of who you were before you were a mom and who you want to be now that you are one. The marriage of these two beautiful versions of yourself will bring you a newfound sense of identity and joy outside of the inevitable highs and lows of motherhood. Reflecting on these topics will allow you to uncover parts of you that you want to highlight and parts that you want to let go of, both of which are valuable in their own ways. We can learn so much about ourselves based on our hopes, dreams, and desires. Awakening ourselves to these topics allows us to move through life with a renewed sense of presence and passion. When we are attuned to what we want in life, we can begin to manifest our vision.

I am so thankful that you have trusted me to walk with you on this journey to process your emotions, uncover your needs, and form rituals and habits that serve you as you embark on the journey of becoming your best self. I know you can find peace and joy in your daily life alongside the demands of parenting—beyond just going through the motions. You are worthy of a life you genuinely love! You are worthy of a life that embodies joy and gratitude rather than stress and overwhelm. It's time to visualize your dreams and embrace growth on this self-care journey together!

Abigail Dosen

How to Use This Book

The purpose of this journal is to help guide you to your very best self, day by day. The book is symbolically organized into nine chapters because I deeply believe that just as it takes nine months to grow an infant in the womb, it also takes at minimum nine months to dive deeply into the concepts I will introduce to you within these pages.

Please do not rush your journey. When you allow yourself to be truly present with your mental, emotional, and physical needs and take the proper time to make lifestyle shifts toward the woman you have always imagined, you will feel a sense of satisfaction, and gradual but sustainable changes will occur. Small choices add up to large, lasting changes. This process works best if you move slowly and focus your attention on making each of these changes over the course of not just days, but weeks and months. Eventually, you'll be able to look back on the years and realize that those small daily choices have added up to huge lifestyle shifts that have changed you in a profound way.

When tackling life changes like these, many of us begin with good intentions but move too quickly in the process. If you choose to rush through these chapters and bombard yourself with too much potential change all at once, you're almost certain to become overwhelmed, which can lead to feelings of inadequacy, which can in turn lead to giving up.

Quitting on our goals because they feel too hard or unattainable is a major component of a fixed mindset. A fixed mindset is characterized by the process of becoming set in an unchanging and often-negative thought cycle, which ultimately causes us to get stuck in a proverbial rut. Since we find it so difficult to move out of this mindset, we stay and continue looping in the same internal struggles day in and day out, with minimal changes or growth.

When hard times strike, it is like being stuck boot-deep in a metaphorical pool of mud. If you have a fixed mindset in this moment, you might worry that moving will splatter more mud everywhere, that if you try to move you will only sink in deeper, or that you're already late for where you're going so there is no point trying. You may be tempted to just stand there in hopeless misery, perhaps waiting for someone else to come along and pull you out. This is a fixed mindset.

But the undeniable fact in this scenario is that standing still in misery will never get you closer to freedom—and standing still in the muck of a fixed mindset will never get you closer to your aspirations either.

When we examine our deeper emotions and needs, we can shift away from a fixed mindset that holds our feet firmly where we don't want to be anymore.

So . . .

What do we want instead? We want a growth mindset.

A growth mindset is characterized by the ability and willingness to persevere through challenges to ultimately continue to flourish. This thought process is formed by the genuine belief that we can continue to change the trajectory of our lives through our choices.

Now, you aren't going to sleep better, eat healthier, drink more water, work out to your full capacity, stop yelling at your kids, be impeccably dressed, uncover limitless quiet time, find personal fulfillment in a hobby, and become a rock star at prioritizing adult interactions overnight. I'm overwhelmed just typing that list! So how can we achieve this mountain of goals to create the life that we so desperately crave without sinking back into the mud of our old routines?

Small daily choices, one step at a time.

The growth mindset is only attainable when you provide yourself with tangible, realistic goals over time. By scaffolding your goals, you can see victory during the process, so once you have achieved part of a goal, you can add on further until you are content with the established habit.

This brings us back to the journal you hold in your hands. Complete this journal slowly and intentionally over the course of nine months to see long-lasting results. It will help you move forward from the stage of wishing things were different without an actual plan. It will help you cultivate that growth mindset, make a plan, set concrete goals, and work to achieve them. You're holding your future in your hands, and now all you have to do is commit to being open, honest, vulnerable, and loyal to yourself.

While using this journal, read the words and absorb the ideas. Sit with the discomfort of your unmet needs. Then take action—meet your needs. There is a reason you are reading these words right now; there is a reason you bought this book: something in your life was calling to you. At this point, you might not be sure what that is specifically, but after this process of self-discovery, I am confident that you will know exactly what you need and how to achieve it. You are being called to the fulfilling life that you desire and undoubtedly deserve. Do not sell yourself short or allow excuses to hold you back. The time is now! You are so worthy of the life you aspire to live.

Before diving into the chapters, take some time to work on the three kickoff activities on the following pages.

Chapter Structure

Each of the nine chapters is made up of four parts. In the first part, you'll read about the topic of the chapter in detail, encountering wisdom, food for thought, and real-life stories. Then, each chapter ends with three activities.

Let's Reflect:
In this first activity, you will reflect on what you just read, thinking about it actively instead of passively.

Let's Visualize:
In the second activity, you will start to envision the future you would like for yourself as relates to the chapter topic.

Let's Grow:
In the final activity, you will set tangible goals, track progress, or expand upon the themes of the chapter in a personal way.

Let's Reflect

As you move toward creating the life that you have always dreamed of, it's vital to understand what that actually means to you. By brainstorming different words that align with your vision, you can find the clarity you need to determine your motivations for making changes. Circle or underline any words that stand out to you as being important in the life you would like to create. You may circle as many as you'd like; there is no limit for this exercise.

Abundance	Devotion	Happiness	Meaning
Accountability	Diligence	Harmony	Mindfulness
Achievement	Energy	Honesty	Moderation
Adventure	Enthusiasm	Imagination	Nature
Appreciation	Faith	Independence	Openness
Authenticity	Flexibility	Integrity	Optimism
Awe	Flow	Joy	Order
Balance	Freedom	Kindness	Originality
Belonging	Focus	Learning	Passion
Calm	Generosity	Liveliness	Patience
Courage	Grace	Logic	Peace
Creativity	Gratitude	Love	Playfulness
Depth	Growth	Mastery	Presence

Prosperity	Service	Teamwork	Variety
Quality	Simplicity	Thoughtfulness	Vitality
Recognition	Sincerity	Tradition	Vigor
Reflection	Skill	Tranquility	Vision
Resilience	Spontaneity	Trust	Warmth
Respect	Strength	Understanding	Wisdom
Richness	Structure	Unity	Wonder
Rituals	Success	Uniqueness	Worth
Serenity	Talent	Usefulness	Zest

Do you have any words to add to the list? Write them on the lines below.

_____   _____

_____   _____

_____   _____

_____   _____

_____   _____

_____   _____

Let's Visualize

Choose four words from the previous activity that align most significantly with your vision for life. In the spaces provided, describe why each word calls to you.

Word: _____

Why would you like to embody this word? _____

_____

_____

How would you like to embody this word? _____

_____

_____

Word: _____

Why would you like to embody this word? _____

_____

_____

How would you like to embody this word? _____

_____

_____

You are so worthy of the life you aspire to live.

Word: _____

Why would you like to embody this word? _____

_____

_____

How would you like to embody this word? _____

_____

_____

Word: _____

Why would you like to embody this word? _____

_____

_____

How would you like to embody this word? _____

_____

_____

Let's Grow

From your list of four words from the previous activity, choose just one that will be your guide over the next nine months. This word should be able to encompass your "why" fully and should be a quick reminder when you are feeling a bit lost and want to come back to full presence.

Your word: _____

Why does this individual word stand out so strongly to you? _____

_____

_____

_____

_____

_____

_____

_____

_____

_____

This week, recall your word in difficult as well as happy moments. Consider putting your word on a sticky note in a place where you will see it each morning, like your bathroom mirror, so you are visually reminded of your why as you begin each day. At the end of the week, answer the questions on the facing page.

How did this word guide you through hard moments? _____

_____

_____

_____

_____

_____

_____

_____

_____

How did this word show up in the great moments? _____

_____

_____

_____

_____

_____

_____

_____

_____

| 1 |

Self-Love

Unpacking Self-Care and Mom Guilt

What is self-care? I know so many people who would instantly say spa days, a bubble bath in the evening, extended time away with friends, or a date night with their significant other, just to name a few examples.

And yes, those are all important aspects of self-care, but it's also essential to recognize that a huge part of self-care consists of meeting our basic daily needs. When we forget to acknowledge our foundational needs, we miss out on the opportunity to flourish on a daily basis, and we're consistently left feeling defeated very quickly, even after a larger self-care activity.

On the other hand, if we fixate on only the simple things, we can be left feeling underappreciated or unfulfilled. Once we have mastered focusing on our smaller basic needs, we can turn our attention to more-complex forms of self-care. The balance between these two types of self-care really allows us to feel wholly cared for and revitalized.

"Love yourself first and everything else falls into line. You really have to love yourself to get anything done in this world."

—LUCILLE BALL

In this chapter, we'll focus on unpacking the varying levels of self-care, which will allow us to distinguish which needs are calling for our attention at any one time so we can nurture ourselves more fully on the path of genuine self-love. I break these needs down into four different levels: basic physical needs, personal and mental needs, social needs, and support needs. These needs can be intertwined, so we may notice that one subset may benefit when another is being nurtured.

In order to fine-tune this concept, I like to think of our needs as that of a large tree. Just as a tree needs strong roots to grow, we as humans rely on a solid foundation of grounded, daily practices to truly thrive. That said, without branches, a tree is just a stick in the mud, so we can't forget about the outward forms of care that allow us to figuratively spread our branches. Imagine yourself gazing upward at an expansive tree. Notice the vastness of the branches and leaves and begin to appreciate the true depth of the tree. What started as a small seedling has become an enormous symbol of strength and vitality held firm by mighty roots. After we foster our foundation by caring for our basic physical needs, we can turn our attention to the deeper mental and emotional needs we all have within our hearts and minds. Just as the tree becomes lush with foliage, we, too, will grow in depth and stand tall in our purpose.

Before we can dive into the specifics of the different levels of self-care, however, we must dedicate some space to the draining concept you probably know of as "mom guilt." I define mom

It's important to be aware of when you feel the urge to put yourself last.

guilt as a malevolent internal voice that tries to convince mothers that we are less deserving of the space, service, and rest that we so willingly provide for the people around us. Mom guilt places entirely unrealistic expectations and ideologies onto our shoulders, thereby preventing us from stepping into a place of peace, acceptance, and love.

Often, we fail to realize that these gigantic expectations are forms of self-sabotage that stem from the desire to "do it all" or to place higher value on others' needs compared to your own. When we face mom guilt head on, we can beat the voice within and instead focus our attention on all the beautiful ways we can show up for the people in our lives without sacrificing ourselves in the process.

Mom guilt can manifest in any of the four levels of needs, so it's important to be aware of when you feel the urge to put yourself last. Sure, sometimes it's a great gesture to think of another above yourself, but not when it's constantly done to the detriment of your physical or emotional self. Recognizing what triggers mom guilt in your mind will allow you to break through your resistance to self-love and to form a plan to show yourself true compassion. You cannot have the life you desire with this guilt hanging over your head. You exist as a living, breathing, unique human being, and you are worthy.

In the early stages of my life as a mom, I struggled desperately with mom guilt, so much so that I would rarely accept

help and often thought it was an attack on my abilities. Eventually I realized I was wrong in my analysis and that my people genuinely wanted to help me. I also started to realize that I needed to speak up for myself and give a voice to my needs. About four months into my role as a stay-at-home mom after my first daughter was born, the world shut down due to COVID-19. At that point, my husband was considered an essential worker, so I was often home alone with the baby. This was an extremely isolating experience, and I'm forever grateful that I had such an amazing husband, family, and group of friends to rely on (albeit through technology) as I navigated the better part of life as a new mom alone in the day-to-day. The silver lining to this experience is that it really gave me the space to consider my priorities in each category of needs. What was I missing most? What was I not missing at all? This is the first step in crushing mom guilt: taking the time to examine your needs.

As I moved forward in this chapter of life, I was able to set some foundational habits in motion. I started a small journaling practice that has now built up into an important reflective piece of my mornings. I made taking care of myself physically through movement a priority and figured out how to make that work within the confines of my own home, especially since Ohio weather doesn't always cooperate with outdoor activities. My husband and I learned how to openly communicate our needs and expectations for how our household is run, which helped us move past quiet resentment and into the "let's talk through this and form a solution" style of teamwork. I was also able to daydream about what I wanted to do once the world opened back up.

Despite the fear and uncertainty that plagued the globe, this was a time of personal reflection for me. We shut our doors and I formed a plan for the mom that I dreamt of becoming. When things did open back up to the new normal, I found that the people-pleasing tendencies I used to have had become much weaker. I was able to better prioritize my own needs and the needs of my family because I realized that if our family unit was not in harmony, then our life was in chaos. I had worked on meeting those smaller basic needs for months on end, and now it was time to incorporate some of the larger needs back into our lives. This time, though, I could work on that with the confidence to unapologetically put myself and our family first.

Another step in the quest to eliminate mom guilt requires you to use your empathetic skills. Whenever you feel the edges of guilt creeping in, ask yourself, *What if a friend of mine was in this position?* Let's say your friend is in desperate need of some new daily-use T-shirts, but she feels guilty spending money on herself rather than using that money on her children. Would you ever encourage your friend to continue wearing her threadbare T-shirts so she could purchase the latest Paw Patrol car? Absolutely not. That sounds a little ridiculous, right? But I have honestly felt mom guilt over this exact situation! Think of some times when you have experienced mom guilt, and then ask yourself, Why do we hold ourselves to a different standard than the other people in our lives? Why do we consistently have this urge to put ourselves at the tail end of the priority list?

Another useful step in the service of curbing mom guilt is to envision your own child in the future. When a situation occurs and they feel conflicted and guilty, would you tell them to continue to sacrifice every need of theirs in the name of love? No. Let's look at another concrete example: Imagine your child is a parent and an opportunity arises for them to go away for a weekend with their closest friends. They have been desperate to connect with their group of friends for some time, but life has gotten in the way until now. Your adult child is clearly excited to go, but they are conflicted because they don't want to leave the childcare up to their spouse for a few days or spend the money for the trip solo rather than including the entire family. Do you encourage them to stay home and skip the trip? Do you agree with their mom guilt trying to convince them that this is selfish? No. You support them in their desire to meet a personal need for social connection!

Self-care prioritizes the self, but it is not selfish.

Remind yourself of these few truths: you are worthy of being cherished and nurtured, you have value as a human being, and your needs matter.

So, the next time you are feeling mom guilt, please take it as an opportunity to talk to yourself from a place of loving kindness. Imagine how you might talk to a close friend or your child in the future. Remind yourself of these truths: you are worthy of being cherished and nurtured, you have value as a human being, your needs matter, and you would not deny the needs of a person you love, so hold yourself to the same standard.

Now that you've read a good deal about mom guilt, it's time for a quick check-in. When was the last time you felt good in your skin? When was the last time you felt nurtured and cared for? As mothers, we are often told that it's our natural instinct to always put our children first, but have you been doing this at the risk of your own well-being? Do not let mom guilt convince you that you have to be last in line. Of course our children have genuine needs that they rely on us to meet, and we should not ignore that fact, but you also have genuine needs that you rely on yourself to meet. Please do not ignore *that* fact.

Speaking of genuine needs, it's time to return to the four levels of needs that I brought up earlier and delve into them in more detail.

LEVEL 1: Basic Physical Needs

Basic physical needs include nourishing your body with high-quality food and drink, getting proper rest in the form of slowing down and adequate sleep, and personal hygiene habits that allow you to feel beautiful and restored.

Meeting your basic day-to-day physical needs allows you to feel content, calm, and grounded. Eating well-balanced meals and staying hydrated, getting enough quality sleep, feeling proud of your self-image, embracing personal and quiet time, and moving your body better equip you to handle the hard, often-overstimulating parts of parenting and to soak in the lovely parts. This will let you move from surviving to thriving.

LEVEL 2: Personal and Mental Needs

Personal and mental needs include discovering your identity and individual value through creativity and hobbies (not exclusively through work), caring for your mental health and well-being, and cultivating a good mindset.

When you move beyond the "me last" mindset, you will be able to tap into the many opportunities for creativity and fulfillment that foster individuality and a positive sense of self. When you break free of the passive instinct to lose yourself in motherhood, you pave the way for contentment and joy.

When you break free of the passive instinct to lose yourself in motherhood, you pave the way for contentment and joy.

LEVEL 3: Social Needs

"Social needs" means connecting with others in the ways that best fit our individual level of introversion or extroversion. This will look different for everyone, because some people recharge socially by attending a large gathering while others feel a stronger benefit from having a one-on-one chat with a friend.

As human beings, we're hardwired to have human connections, so when we lack meaningful social interactions in our life, we feel the isolation profoundly. In a world of social media and instantaneous modes of communication, it's important to note that just because you are talking to someone doesn't mean you are genuinely connecting with them. The feeling of being alone in a crowded room is more apparent than ever in our society, so genuine social experiences are more important than ever before.

LEVEL 4: Support Needs

They say it takes a village—and it does—but the village of today looks way different than the villages of the past. Nowadays, many of us need to make our own support system, which is no easy task, but support in mothering is vital whether it comes from blood family, chosen family, friends, or all the above.

Our modern world provides unique challenges to the concept of village parenting, and often comparison to other parents' villages can bring you a lot of frustration. Accepting the support that is readily available to you and seeking out support that is realistic to attain—and suited to your individual life and needs—is crucial to creating a successful village of your own.

Let's Reflect

Mothering is a wonderful experience, but it can also be overstimulating and draining if we forget to pay attention to the different levels of our needs. Our most basic needs must be addressed, or we'll be trying to run around each day on a half-full tank. When we start by addressing the little details, then the big forms of self-care stop feeling so desperately needed. We can still enjoy being pampered and look forward to things like a mani-pedi, but when we take care of the smaller aspects of self-care first, it will help eliminate the feeling that we are crawling tiredly toward whatever elaborate event we put on the calendar for me time.

Furthermore, a cravings-based state of mind like this makes it all too easy to forget the good things in our daily lives and instead lock ourselves into the mindset of "I'll feel better after X." Yes, we do feel the immediate relief of a massage or a pedicure, but, shocker, once it's over, we often go right back to how we were feeling before: defeated, exhausted, and all-around burnt out. Focusing on basic needs and then moving to our personal, mental, social, and support needs is truly a recipe for success!

For this activity, check always, sometimes, or never for each prompt. This exercise works best when you are wholly honest, so don't hold back. It also helps to consider these prompts generally throughout the course of a week or month as you respond, rather than pinned to a specific day. Your answers are your starting point for working toward self-love and self-care!

ALWAYS	SOMETIMES	NEVER	
◯	◯	◯	I wake up feeling refreshed and ready for the day.
◯	◯	◯	I have enough downtime to decompress.
◯	◯	◯	My body feels strong and healthy.
◯	◯	◯	I feel proud of my physical appearance/clothing.
◯	◯	◯	I eat three well-balanced meals a day.
◯	◯	◯	I take time for myself without feeling mom guilt.
◯	◯	◯	I have time to pursue my hobbies and interests.
◯	◯	◯	My stress levels feel manageable.
◯	◯	◯	I speak up when I need more help or support.
◯	◯	◯	I take time to reflect and process my feelings/emotions.
◯	◯	◯	I spend quality time with my friends.
◯	◯	◯	When I feel overwhelmed, I take steps to make myself feel better.
◯	◯	◯	My support system is available and helpful.
◯	◯	◯	I am pleased with my level of exercise/physical movement.
◯	◯	◯	My body feels cared for physically in terms of cleanliness and health.
◯	◯	◯	I have a healthy balance with my digital devices/social media.
◯	◯	◯	The breakdown of housework and chores in my home feels fair.
◯	◯	◯	I feel cared for, nourished, and loved.

Let's Visualize

Visualization is a powerful tool that allows you to uncover your deeper desires, which sets the stage for making them real. The five-senses visualization practice featured here will encourage you to consider your goals through each of the senses, giving you a clear, detailed, and tangible picture of how you envision your life. Complete the sentences below to unlock your life's vision.

Basic Physical Needs

When my basic physical needs are met, I feel:

_____

_____

When my basic physical needs are met, I see:

_____

_____

When my basic physical needs are met, I hear:

_____

_____

When my basic physical needs are met, I smell:

_____

_____

When my basic physical needs are met, I taste:

_____

_____

Personal and Mental Needs

When my personal and mental needs are met, I feel:

_____

_____

When my personal and mental needs are met, I see:

_____

_____

When my personal and mental needs are met, I hear:

_____

_____

When my personal and mental needs are met, I smell:

_____

_____

When my personal and mental needs are met, I taste:

_____

_____

When we start by addressing the little details, then the big forms of self-care stop feeling so desperately needed.

Social Needs

When my social needs are met, **I feel**:

_____

_____

When my social needs are met, **I see**:

_____

_____

When my social needs are met, **I hear**:

_____

_____

When my social needs are met, **I smell**:

_____

_____

When my social needs are met,
I taste:

_____

_____

Support Needs

When my support needs are met, **I feel**:

_____

_____

When my support needs are met, **I see**:

_____

_____

When my support needs are met, **I hear**:

_____

_____

When my support needs are met,
I smell:

_____

_____

When my support needs are met,
I taste:

_____

_____

Let's Grow

As you consider your responses to the different levels of needs, you will begin to anticipate which areas are lacking your love and attention. When you recognize an unmet need in the moment (often in the form of stress, overstimulation, irritability, sadness, or angst), you can use the five-finger senses practice to evaluate your needs.

In the five-finger senses practice, each finger represents one of the five senses and is used to check in on your status and make changes related to what you can touch, see, hear, smell, and taste. In the heat of a difficult moment, ask yourself the following questions, counting them off on your fingers.

What do I need to feel right now?
Maybe you need to feel your bottom sitting down in a chair for a moment, or to change out of an uncomfortable piece of clothing.

What do I need to see right now?
You may need to see nothing—close your eyes.

What do I need to hear right now?
Is it too loud and chaotic around you? You might need to hear less. Turn the TV off or move to a different room.

What do I need to smell right now?
Light a calming candle or run a diffuser to tap into your sense of smell. Stepping outside to breathe in the fresh air can be a great reset too.

What do I need to taste right now?
Consider whether you are hungry or thirsty, or even just have a lingering bad taste in your mouth. Eat or drink something if so.

There you go—you can quickly meet some basic needs to help you decompress.

If, as you are taking this moment, you are recognizing that a deeper social, personal, mental, or support need is not being met, this practice can be very beneficial as a journaling prompt. Refer back to your visualizations in the previous activity to check in on where there is a disconnect between your goals and what is actually happening in the present. Then grab a journal and write out your five-finger senses responses as they relate to (and possibly contradict) your goals.

This month, use the below symbols and calendar to track each day that you notice you have met one or more of the four levels of needs.

Basic Physical Needs	Personal and Mental Needs	Social Needs	Support Needs
$\checkmark$	♡	😊	✩

1

2

3

4

5

6

7

8

9

10

11

12

13

14

15

16

17

18

19

20

21

22

23

24

25

26

27

28

29

30

|2|

Nourishment

Embracing Mealtimes as a Source of Fuel and Loving Kindness

For busy moms, having a well-balanced meal can sometimes feel unattainable, rushed, or like a complete afterthought, but getting proper nutrition is vital to keeping our systems working as they should in both mind and body.

When we move through our days, it's tempting to ignore the impact that food has on us. As we grab a granola bar on the way out the door or shovel a spoonful of mac and cheese into our mouths while standing over the stove, it may seem like harmless behavior, but eventually our body will speak its needs to us in one way or another.

When you think about your relationship with meals, start by asking yourself, *Do I actually eat three well-balanced and nutritious meals a day?* Or are you like me in the past, eating whatever I could shove down in one minute or less because I was "too busy" to sit? In this chapter, we will work through the importance of nourishing your body from a place of loving kindness.

"The food you eat can be either the safest and most powerful form of medicine or the slowest form of poison."

—ANN WIGMORE

W e already know that what we put into our bodies has a direct impact on our physical well-being, but it also plays a huge role in our moods and energy levels. As tempting as some of my favorite snack foods are, I can't deny that I am often left feeling lethargic and irritable when I race through a meal with only a handful of this or that rather than having a full meal consisting of healthy items. I'm sure you can relate.

An added benefit to focusing on feeding your body the fuel it requires to function well is that you will be modeling this habit for your children. I know this is a book about you as an individual, but it can't hurt to use your children's future as a source of motivation; they will see and hopefully follow your example of a healthy relationship with your body and nutrition.

I have a true story to share with you that will help drive home a lesson that took me way too long to learn.

"Stay in your seat! We sit in our seats until we're all finished eating. Please sit down!" I repeated for what felt like the eight-hundredth time that week.

My daughter Mia happily climbed back onto her booster and dunked another bite of her waffle into syrup, only to hop back down within a minute. *Why can't you just sit down when it's breakfast (or lunch or dinner)?* I thought to myself. Frustrating, right? I was begging her to just sit down to eat, and then *afterward* she could go play or climb or run or do whatever. But if she would only just sit. and. eat. the. food.

Where did Mia learn this up and down, up and down on repeat every single meal? I wondered as I stood up to refill the milk cup, grab my coffee, check my phone, wash a couple dishes, wipe up crumbs, and *oh, I think I just heard the laundry buzz.*

Well, shoot . . . It was me, wasn't it? (Insert melting-face emoji here.)

After I had this fateful realization, I started paying attention to when I actually sat down to eat meals with my kids. If I had a sticker chart for staying in my seat, then breakfast and lunch were habitually a total failure; I'd be peeling stickers off the chart to give them back, it was that bad! Dinner was a little iffy too, but I gave myself a 33% score just to boost my confidence a bit.

So what was the key difference between breakfast and lunch versus dinner? My husband could tell you— one of his pet peeves is my "one more thing" nature. I can't sit still. It's like *If You Give a Mouse a Cookie*, mom-style. Let's call it *If You Leave a Paper Towel on the Counter.*

If You Leave a Paper Towel on the Counter: A Memoir

If you leave a paper towel on the counter, then I'll have to wipe up that spill. When I wipe up the spill, I'll need to toss the towel in the garbage. On the way to the trash, I'll step on a crumb. That crumb (it was actually 5,892 crumbs, but who's counting) will need to be vacuumed, so I'll grab the vacuum. When I go to grab the vacuum, I'll trip over shoes in the mudroom. As I straighten the shoes, I'll spot the open diaper bag and realize it's out of wipes. As I go to grab the wipes, I'll pass the kitchen and see my lovely family sitting down to dinner. I'll look at my husband's increasingly frustrated face and realize that reloading the diaper bag can wait, because the truly important thing at this moment is . . . I really have to pee.

I wish I could say that this happened once and I got better at sitting still during meals, but sadly, it didn't. It took my husband, Tony, getting seriously annoyed with me and a frank conversation about dinnertimes to make a difference. We made a rule that every night we'd sit down to eat together as a family—without phones—to enjoy our dinner. This was a start.

I'm now working on sitting for breakfast and lunch too, because this new habit we established for dinner has really shown some benefits. One benefit, of course, is modeling sitting down to eat for my kids; this has minimized instances when syrup fingers start to wander around my entire open-concept kitchen and living room and make me want to scream.

But the more important benefit is that it lets me enjoy the nourishment I'm providing my body instead of wolfing it down like a teenaged boy after football two-a-days. It's a form of self-respect to prepare yourself *actual* meals and sit down in an *actual* seat to eat them. You are worth more than a forkful of soggy, half-eaten (and most likely licked) waffles and three stray blueberries washed down with the backwash from your toddler's cup of milk. And don't forget that a meal like that is typically "enjoyed" over the sink while simultaneously washing up the breakfast dishes.

The moral of the story is to pay attention to whether or not you're sitting down to eat your food. You're worth a high-quality, fresh meal consumed in an actual seat. Once you make it a point to sit to eat for every single meal (yes—all of them!), you're going to:

1. **Feel fuller and more satisfied.** You'll actually have more than a bite or two of your child's rejected scraps! An added bonus is that you'll probably get sick less often too, because I'm sure at least half of you reading this currently have a boogery child.

2. **Feel valuable, cared for, and energized.** Just as feeding a loved one a meal makes them feel this way, feeding yourself a meal can do the same.

3. **Feel the slightest bit calmer at mealtimes.** Operating on an empty stomach during tiger—I mean, toddler—feeding time is not easy, and trying to do this without your own needs being met is even harder. Yes, being hangry is a legitimate problem.

4. **Feel like a role model.** I'm not making promises, because children are about as predictable as the weather in the Midwest (if you're not from around here, that means not at all predictable), but they really are always watching, and they might learn something good.

5. **Feel less overstimulated and make fewer errors.** I've broken a dish or two in my haste while multitasking before I started to recognize that moving faster doesn't always equal completing things faster. Being able to focus your attention on the task at hand will encourage a sense of peace that results in less breakage!

To wrap up this chapter on nourishment, I want to take some time to unpack the "they really are always watching" statement I made above, through a flashback to long before I was a mother. This story still strikes a chord with me to this day, especially now that I am a mom to three little girls, and I think it could help you too.

Enter scene: a young Abby, fresh out of college, in her first full-time teaching job as a middle-school English and reading teacher. On this particular day, it was the worst-case scenario: bad weather and indoor recess, when teachers have to stay in their classrooms to monitor the kids.

I had somehow managed to waste the first half of the lunch period doing who knows what, and now I had to eat my lunch with the kids in the room, so I sat down at my desk. (Kudos to me for sitting down to eat, though!) I had a meager salad and not much else. A group of the middle-school girls were hanging by my desk chitchatting when one delivered the comment that floored me: "Miss Cole, you never eat enough. Your lunch is always so tiny if you have one."

It's a form of self-respect to prepare yourself actual meals and sit down in an actual seat to eat them.

She was right. I wasn't eating nearly enough, partly because I was constantly trying to multitask, and partly because I wasn't paying attention to my own basic needs. This moment made me realize it wasn't only about me. These young, impressionable girls who looked up to me noticed my choices. They saw me racing around, ignoring my physical needs and barely feeding my body. From that day forward, I made a point to pack well-balanced, full lunches, and I made a vow that if I ever became a mom, especially to girls, I would show my body love by providing it with adequate nutrition.

Enter scene: my three beautiful little girls.

It might seem like no big deal to eat just a few bites of lunch until your stomach isn't growling anymore because there are other things to do, but they notice.

Sit down and eat. For you. For them.

Let's Reflect

When thinking about the hectic mealtimes in my past, I began to understand that the real reason I struggled with making myself consistent meals was twofold. First of all, I found that after making my kids breakfast and lunch during the day, I often felt tired and had no desire to make an additional meal for myself. In these cases, I'd settle for something fast and convenient, but not necessarily healthy or filling. Second, I realized that I had horrible decision fatigue at mealtimes. I was tired of making choices, so I'd reach for anything simple or premade. Unfortunately, most of these options left me feeling, to be frank, hangry. I had to find a way to make my meals easy, fast, and as decision-free as possible. This is when I shifted toward meal planning in advance and having items ready to go, whether it was all-in-one containers or simply that the ingredients were right there ready to use.

When it came to dinner, the problem was exacerbated because I felt even more tired and decision-fatigued than at the other two mealtimes. Dinner was accompanied by a hefty dose of mom guilt any time I started trying to rush around to toss something together after my husband got home from work.

Once I stopped letting the mom guilt get in my way, my husband and I were able to form a plan where we both participated in coming up with the idea for each dinner along with participating in the actual preparation of said meal. Now we work together consistently, which has largely released the pressures that were previously all on my shoulders. We made a shared Instagram saved folder where my husband and I could both flag recipes, and we head into each week with a plan for our dinners. We work together to form grocery lists, pick up groceries with our local grocer's drive-up option, or go to the store to shop for our own items. The mental load is balanced because I am not solely in charge of the meal decisions and the shopping. Sharing this responsibility between the two of us has become such a beneficial practice.

For this exercise, consider your average mealtime experience. Then jot down your responses in the boxes below.

	BREAKFAST	LUNCH	DINNER
What do you eat most often?			
What do you drink most often?			
Where do you sit?			
How long is the mealtime?			

What is working at any/all of your meals? _____

_____

_____

What needs to change at any/all of your meals?_____

_____

_____

Let's Visualize

Envision what mealtimes would ideally look like for you in a best-case scenario. Brainstorm a list of potential breakfast, lunch, and dinner options that you'd like to try.

BREAKFAST	LUNCH	DINNER

Use the space below to visualize how your future self will show up for mealtimes.

BREAKFAST: What do you eat and drink, where do you sit, how long is the meal, and how do you feel?

_____

_____

_____

_____

_____

LUNCH: What do you eat and drink, where do you sit, how long is the meal, and how do you feel?

_____

_____

_____

_____

_____

DINNER: What do you eat and drink, where do you sit, how long is the meal, and how do you feel?

_____

_____

_____

_____

_____

Let's Grow

Choose one meal to focus on this week and jot down a plan for the week in the chart below. Along the side, create a list of items you need to pick up from the grocery store to set yourself up for success. Make a point to eat the meal you planned in the location you previously visualized. At the end of the week, share your response to the reflection questions on the facing page.

	MEAL IDEA	SHOPPING LIST
Monday		
Tuesday		
Wednesday		
Thursday		
Friday		
Saturday		
Sunday		

How was this activity meaningful for you this week?

_____

_____

_____

_____

_____

_____

_____

_____

_____

How can you continue to prioritize fueling your body with nourishing food on a regular basis?

_____

_____

_____

_____

_____

_____

_____

_____

_____

_____

Mindful Rest

Prioritizing Adequate Rest with Intentional Habits

In the world of parenting, rest can sometimes feel like a paradox. We desperately need high-quality sleep to feel like our best selves, but we stay up late into the night to steal some "me time." We find a quiet pocket of time to rest during the day, but rather than sitting down to take advantage of the peace, we rush around to knock out chores or catch up on our to-do list.

Sometimes, our busy minds keep us up later than we intend with endless loops of thoughts about what we didn't accomplish that day or what we need to accomplish the following day.

These are just some examples of many experiences surrounding rest, or lack thereof, that I've heard from countless moms. In this chapter, we're going to dive into how we personally rest and recharge to discover how we can form a solid plan for high-quality restorative practices and sleep habits going forward.

"Courage doesn't always roar. Sometimes courage is the little voice at the end of the day that says, I'll try again tomorrow."

—MARY ANNE RADMACHER

Trying to maintain a healthy lifestyle and peaceful mind is much harder when you're constantly tired, and sometimes simply sleeping for the recommended daily amount is not enough to fulfill your rest needs. You also need solid downtime during the day to mentally restore calm presence. As we dive into the topic of rest, it's important that you take a peek into how you're using your time throughout the whole day, not just your sleeping hours.

For example, if you are struggling to maintain a consistent bedtime, you must uncover the root of what is preventing you from establishing this healthy routine. Are you trying to get everything done solo? Are you doom-scrolling on your phone for longer than you realize? Are you ruminating on the day? Are you setting unrealistic expectations for what has to be accomplished in a day and eating up your rest time to achieve them? The answers to these questions will help you determine what's holding you back from feeling energized and ready to take on a new day after what on paper might be a "full" night of sleep.

Let's start setting you up for nights of high-quality, deep sleep that is completely superior to the quality of rest you've probably been achieving up till now.It's going to take discipline, but I know you can do it. I see this as a threefold approach.

1. **Genuinely consider how much sleep you need to feel fully rested.** This will allow you to form a reasonable plan to get yourself as close to that amount as is realistic in your current life. Yeah, nine hours of sleep with a gradual wake-up time of around 8:30 a.m. would be my ideal, but I do have children and can almost guarantee that when 6:30 a.m. rolls around, they're ready to play Play-Doh and have the energy to run a full marathon. With that knowledge, I can form a routine that accommodates their wake-up time and still allows me to get proper rest. Maybe right now, I have to go to bed closer to 10:00 p.m. to make sure I feel rested when I wake up in the morning. My night-owl tendencies would love to stay up until 11:30 p.m. or midnight, but that simply is a bad choice for me at this phase of my life.

2. Account for the relationship between nights and mornings. Your morning routine is just as important as your nighttime routine in regard to getting the rest you need. When we have a structured morning routine that sets us up for success, we can fully rest at night and not begin our day with the hectic rushing around that almost always induces a fight-or-flight response and higher levels of stress. Figure out a set of tasks and an order for them, and then try to stick to it so that you're not wasting your early-morning energy.

Your morning routine is just as important as your nighttime routine in regard to getting the rest you need.

3. **Use the quiet time before bed for maximum value instead of unintentionally wasting it.** Have you ever been binging a show or scrolling on TikTok only to realize that literal hours have passed? I've been there! There is extreme worth in the quiet hours of the night—that time when the kids are asleep—when they're used to fill your cup in mindful ways instead of mind-numbing ways, and it's up to you to purposefully monitor how you're using this time.

I want to spend a good part of this chapter focusing on item number 3 of this list, as it's something that I've seen crop up often in fellow moms. Raise your hand if you stayed up way later than normal so you could have some quiet time to yourself to mindlessly scroll on your phone, so you could mentally escape a day that so entirely took it out of you that you cannot even think. Go ahead, raise your hand.

I know I'm not alone in this habit, and neither are you. But do you know what makes the next difficult day even harder? Attempting to function on minimal sleep all over again!

Raising kids (of any age) is hard, full stop. They are inevitably going to be needy, whine and cry, throw colossal tantrums, want us to play all the games, ask a million questions, need to be dropped off and picked up all over the city, ask for help with homework, and the list goes on. Trying to take care of these nonstop demands can feel miserable when you're exhausted. There's a reason for the ongoing joke featuring a completely spent parent offering to take their child's nap for them. We are tired!

When you're in the trenches of raising children, it can feel like the only time you have for yourself is the beloved post-bedtime quiet hour. It can feel like it's worth it to ignore your basic sleep needs to squeeze out more of that time from your day. I hear these refrains from moms all the time: "I just needed to scroll and not think" and "I am so tired I can't *do* anything—scrolling on my phone just lets me zone out." It might seem like the scrolling is helping you decompress, but when I started to get really honest with myself about this habit, I realized that it wasn't helping me, it was hurting me. I kept telling myself that to decompress, I needed to do something mindless, but what I really needed was to do something mindful.

Mindful? After a chaotic, exhausting day? You want me to use my mind more? Yes, I do.

I want you to work on the things that make you tick. I want you to figure out what fills your cup and use the quiet time for these activities. They can be mindful and stimulating or mindful and relaxing. No two women will have the same activities, and the quiet period in which you do them isn't going to look the same every day. Some days, reading or writing fills me up, and other days, taking a big bubble bath fills my cup. Occasionally, I enjoy diving into a new TV series or watching a movie with my husband. You may want to sit down and color or work on a craft. The point is that you have to get serious about what you're doing during this precious time and analyze whether or not it serves you or simply numbs you, because there's a huge difference between the

Figure out what fills your cup and use the quiet time for these activities.

two. And, don't forget, sometimes the best choice when your kids go to bed is for you to also hit the hay! Not every evening needs to have its special hour of me time. Listen to your body—it might be telling you what you need.

The fact is, the quiet hour when everyone else is sleeping is a beautiful time when it's used properly. When used improperly, it reinforces the narrative that being a mother has to *always* be exhausting or unfulfilling and that there is *never* enough time. When it's used properly, it not only eliminates a chronic problem plaguing everyone—not just mothers—in society but also provides an opportunity for your alone time to truly become you time—time in which you enrich, nourish, and prioritize yourself.

Before we get into the journaling activities for this chapter, I have one more related topic to cover. Recognizing your full potential for rest and recovery requires determining what needs to get done each day and how to efficiently complete these tasks. We all have responsibilities, but can you sort these tasks so your evenings aren't a race around the house until you pass out from exhaustion? If you're struggling, I have a suggestion for you . . .

There are certain tasks, such as laundry, that I now typically refuse to do when my children are sleeping. In general, household chores are time consuming and often feel overwhelming. I have decided that I want my kids to not only witness the effort that goes into these tasks but to also be a part of the upkeep. They can't witness or pitch in if they are sleeping when the chores are magically completed! Sure, my four-year-old doesn't put the laundry away quite right or vacuum the rugs the same way I would, but she's learning a valuable skill—teamwork—and a valuable truth: that a comfortable home only exists because of chores.

For a long time, dinner cleanup was the bane of my existence. Then I adopted the "work smarter, not harder" mentality. My two older daughters (ages four and two) love to help out, and I wasn't tapping into that resource. Once I realized this, I got them involved; they are now responsible for clearing their dishes from the table and tossing any trash into the garbage. For now, they set them on the counter, and my husband and I alternate who's washing the dishes or who is wiping up the floor, the table, and the one-year-old. My four-year-old has also begun to express interest in loading and unloading the dishwasher. Go ahead, roll your eyes, I would have too! But, honestly, as you scaffold teamwork, kids start to realize that they are helpful members of the family and that they have duties too. Now I'm no longer cleaning up the kitchen alone while I grumble under my breath that it isn't fair, *and* I have some extra time back because many hands make light work! By the time my kids go to bed, *our* chores are already done. They rest, and I rest.

Let's Reflect

For this activity, rate how often you do the following statements, as honestly as possible. Put 0 for rarely, 1 for sometimes, and 2 for always. When you're done, tally up your results get the result for your personal mindful rest and recovery status.

RARELY	SOMETIMES	ALWAYS
0	1	2

_____ I have a consistent nighttime routine.

_____ I have a consistent morning routine.

_____ I wake up feeling rested and energetic.

_____ I have a good balance with my devices in the evening.

_____ I have a good balance with my devices in the morning.

_____ I am happy with my nighttime activities after my kids are sleeping.

_____ I go to bed at a time that feels adequate to me.

_____ I wake up at a time that feels adequate to me.

_____ I complete household tasks with my family members.

_____ I plan household tasks so they can be done little by little throughout the week.

0–7 points: It's time to overhaul your rest patterns. Going forward, prioritize getting enough hours of sleep every single day. Start by choosing a bedtime and sticking to it! Set an alarm if you need to, and do not stray from the alarm. And go to bed!

8–16 points: You're smack dab in the middle! You may already have some healthy rest patterns, but oftentimes you're still feeling tired or drained at night or in the morning. A consistent wind-down routine and a set bedtime will help you solidify genuine rest. Try limiting your screen time in the evenings and mornings and using that time for something you enjoy!

17–20 points: You have it (almost) all figured out! We know there's always room to improve, so review any of your 0 or 1 answers. How can you modify your current routine to fine-tune your rest in a mindful and restorative way?

Circle any wind-down techniques that you would be interested in trying:

Meditation	Warm tea	Gratitude list
Reading	Incense/candle	Watching the sunset
Journaling	Stretching	Podcast
Warm bath	Stargazing	Puzzle
Yoga	Meaningful conversation	Adult coloring book

Let's Visualize

As you plan your morning and nighttime routines, consider the following items: what time your children go to bed and wake up on average, how much sleep you need to feel rested, what time would be an ideal locked-in bedtime for you, what time you need to wake up to avoid "rush" stress, and what items you would like to do that don't involve chores or preparation-based tasks.

Describe a nighttime routine that allows for mindful rest to close out your day:

_____

_____

_____

_____

_____

_____

_____

Describe a morning routine that allows you to feel empowered as you kick off your day:

_____

_____

_____

_____

_____

_____

_____

Now that you have brainstormed your intentions for your nighttime and morning routines, let's plan them out in detail. In the charts provided, add the time in the left column and the activity in the right column.

Nighttime Routine

TIME	ACTIVITY

Morning Routine

TIME	ACTIVITY

Let's Grow

This month, make a point to follow your routines as closely as possible. Give yourself a score at the end of each of the four weeks, with the goal of improving your score each week. A perfect 7 in a single week means that you nailed both your morning and nighttime routines every day; a 3.5 might mean that you nailed half of your days or were only a little bit off-routine most days.

WEEK 1:
___/7

WEEK 2:
___/7

WEEK 3:
___/7

WEEK 4:
___/7

How do you feel at bedtime after following your routine?

_____

_____

_____

_____

_____

_____

How do you feel in the mornings after following your routine?

_____

_____

_____

_____

_____

_____

Think about the barriers you encountered that are preventing you from meaningful, restorative practices or from going to bed at a proper time to give yourself full rest. Sometimes, these items are unavoidable—we all have tasks that we need to do or emergencies that come up. Consider if any of your roadblocks can be unblocked with the regular help of another family member to lessen the load, accomplished at a different time, or simplified to be more efficient.

What roadblocks did you encounter during your month?

_____

_____

_____

_____

_____

_____

_____

_____

What are some ways these barriers be addressed as detours instead of roadblocks?

_____

_____

_____

_____

_____

_____

_____

_____

|4|

Personal Appearance

Embracing the Layers of Our Outward Presence with Pride

There are many facets to consider regarding how we feel about personal appearance and how we present ourselves to the world. Oftentimes, we recognize things like basic hygiene, clothing, hair, makeup, and jewelry, but our personal appearance also includes the attitude we present on a daily basis.

When thinking about our personal hygiene, we have to consider not only how we physically cleanse and care for our body, but also how we mentally clear away the dirt.

In this chapter, we'll touch on both physical and mental upkeep in the service of developing habits that will allow us to present faces that feel like they are truly our own to the world. There is no prescription in these pages saying that to care for your personal appearance you must do X, Y, and Z—self-presentation is unique. The goal, rather, is to allow you to figure out what matters to you in terms of presenting *your* self to the world.

"My mission in life is not merely to survive but to thrive; and to do so with some passion, some compassion, some humor, and some style."

—MAYA ANGELOU

Whenever I start to feel a little run down or out of sorts, I reflect on my personal hygiene both physically and mentally. My favorite way to figure out what is lacking for me physically is by imagining that I have a special event like a wedding to attend—usually there are some extra steps I take to feel my absolute best for a wedding. Then I do that routine that day! Yup—wedding-ready on a random Tuesday morning. Don't knock it till you try it.

Nothing pulls me out of a slump faster than really pampering myself with a steamy shower, full-body lotion, blow-drying and styling my hair, a mani-pedi, and, yes, makeup too! I don't go so far as to put on a wedding-guest dress, but you get the picture. A full refresh reminds you that you are a worthy human being, and the care that you put into washing, clothing, brushing, and honoring your children should also be reflected in the care that you put into your own body.

As a stay-at-home mom, I don't do this "wedding-ready" process every single day. However, I do take some regular daily steps to make me feel good in my skin. One important thing for me was creating a morning and evening skincare routine. Having this simple, instinctive habit helps me feel pampered in just a few minutes each night and morning. It also sets my day up for success because I do it before my kids wake up, but it's quick! I don't have time for a thirty-minute sheet mask in the morning. (Plus, the couple of times I have tried a sheet mask in front of my kids, the youngest two sobbed uncontrollably until I took it off. I guess they *are* kind of scary looking.)

I've heard this joke one too many times (and experienced it in real life): the kids walk out the door looking adorably perfect with their freshly laundered (and often brand-new) outfits, squeaky clean from the bath, and hair sculpted like they just left the stylist's chair . . . then out walks mom in a wrinkled shirt covered in spit-up and boogers, three-day-old leggings with a questionable

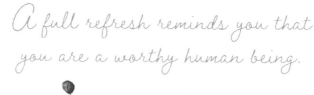

A full refresh reminds you that you are a worthy human being.

hole around the crotch, and sporting a messy bun that may or may not have been washed in the last week. But hey, at least she took a body shower today, right? Nope—that's not gonna fly anymore.

As you consider what you'd like to present as your outward appearance, really think about all the possibilities that this topic encompasses. Here are some ideas to get your gears turning.

Are you regularly brushing and flossing your teeth, or maybe whitening them if you like that?

Have you been caring for your hair? This may include going to regular hair appointments, or maybe you only like a trim once a year.

Do you have a skincare routine? Maybe it's one step, maybe it's ten steps.

Are you rushing through every single shower or are you taking the time to clean yourself lovingly?

How about nail care, eyebrow maintenance, and makeup preferences?

How do certain pieces of clothing in your closet make you feel? Do you have any special jewelry that sparks joy?

All of these items fall under the umbrella of personal presentation, and they are all unique to you! Personal appearance is unique to each mother (and person) to a degree that basic essentials like nourishment and sleep are not.

As you consider these different forms of self-presentation, take note of the activities and habits that no longer make you feel like your best self. Donate clothing that doesn't fit in a way that promotes confidence and joy. Open your medicine cabinet and clear out the expired or unused products. You may begin to realize that something you used to really love no longer serves you, or, just as possibly, you'll recognize the opposite: that you miss something from pre-motherhood and desperately want that back.

I will forever remember a conversation I had with a few family members about the topic of painting your nails as a mom. At this point, I was pregnant with my first daughter, Zoey, and we were talking about how much time it takes to paint your nails, whether it's shellac, gel, quick-dry polish, regular polish, or the glorious treat of actually heading to a nail salon for a full set.

Don't let someone else tell you that you won't have time or energy for whatever self-care item makes you feel your best.

Now, full disclosure, I have always been one to wear nail polish. I think it has something to do with the fact that the school I went to from K-8th grade banned you from having even a clear topcoat on your natural nails (a policy that to this day I cannot understand in the slightest). I felt thoroughly deprived from late August through early June when my nail polish potential was curbed, so, as a grown adult, I guess I'm subconsciously trying to make up for all that lost time.

Pressing on (Get it? Pressing on? Press-on nails? Bad joke, sorry), in this conversation, both of the other moms I was speaking to—who had already given birth to their children—agreed that painting your nails was an impossible thing to keep up with once you had children, and that I would never continue to paint my nails once my baby was born. There would

be absolutely no time for something so lavish as putting a color on my nails, they said with confidence. I was skeptical because, as I mentioned, I really don't like someone telling me that I cannot paint my nails, but I was willing to allow that it was a possibility. Zoey wasn't born yet, so although it was super easy for me to pamper myself with an at-home manicure or head to the salon for a glorious mani-pedi to treat myself in my swollen, uncomfy pregnant state, maybe they were right. Maybe once the baby arrived, I really would have to let go of this little indulgence that I had grown to love. And in the end, what could it hurt to let go of this one little thing?

Once my daughter Zoey was born, I will admit there were moments when I thought, "Ugh, I don't have time for painting my nails anymore!" But what I began to realize is that this one little thing made me feel *so good*! I hated that I'd even considered eliminating this part of my normal personal routine. The truth was, it did take time to sit down and paint my nails, and it still takes time. But the more important truth was that the act of painting my nails made me feel empowered and cared for whether I did it at home (mostly) or headed to a salon for the service (less frequently, but always amazing). Painting my nails is a small part of my personal routine that I decided I could not leave in my pre-mom life because it makes me feel like my best self.

Maybe you have naked nails and you love the look—there's absolutely no judgment here! My point is, we all have our "thing" that falls under the umbrella of taking care of our physical well-being and that might seem a little extra but that actually makes a huge difference to us. Don't give up on your thing! Don't let someone else tell you that you won't have time or energy for whatever self-care item makes you feel your best. To drive this point home, here's a detail I didn't yet mention about the story of this conversation: the only reason those two moms both agreed that nail painting was a waste of precious time that I would surely let fall by the wayside is because painting nails wasn't *their* thing! (And certainly don't let someone else make you feel ashamed of taking time for your thing. These moms didn't, but sometimes people do.)

Do not give up on your thing.

You can have more than one thing too, of course! Prioritize the self-care rituals on your list. These little items add up. Yes, they do take time, but you're worth it. If you aren't feeling fully refreshed from your current personal routine, then it's time to discover what you're skipping in your process. Maybe that something is from your pre-baby life, or maybe it's a brand-new service or product that you want to try. Either way, try to figure out how you can make it a habit.

Now let's turn to the second aspect of your outward presence: your attitude. I can picture those corny classroom posters exclaiming "Attitude is everything!" in big bold colors right now, but let's not discredit that message just because it's a cliche. You can be the best-dressed person in the room or have the most-luscious locks, but there is no denying that one of the most important aspects of your outward presence is how you think and feel. If you're angry or resentful, it will show on your face no matter how much money you spent on a HydraFacial last week. If you feel ashamed of your post-birth body despite wearing your best clothing and a full face of makeup, it will show in your mood and attitude.

It is vital that we clean up our thoughts and minds in the same way we wash our hands with soap: thoroughly and multiple times a day. Life can throw a lot at us, and our brains are just doing their best at processing these curveballs, but we have to help them out!

The first step to "cleansing" your brain is to recognize the emotions you are feeling and accept them as neither good nor bad, but rather neutral. A feeling is in essence a reaction to something that happens. It isn't inherently bad to feel anger, sadness, or frustration; in fact, it's a solid sign that you are alive and capable of feeling a full range of emotions. The problem lies in how we use these emotions to guide our next steps. Remember getting stuck in the mud in chapter 1? Digging your heels in and rooting down in negative feelings is not going to help you move forward. You have to accept and sit

One of the most important aspects of your outward appearance is how you think and feel.

When you allow yourself to process your emotions in an empowering way, you can begin to exude an attitude of peace, confidence, and contentment.

with any emotion so you can process the way you're truly feeling, hopefully understand why you are feeling that way, and then make a plan or decision to move forward productively. A few great techniques for understanding a deep emotion include journaling, calling a friend, talking to a therapist, or meditating. There are also lots of great books out there that can help you notice patterns in the way you react to challenges.

The second step to "cleansing" your brain is to form a response plan. Once you have understood why you feel the way you feel, you can take the necessary steps to make changes. You

can't control your feelings, but you can control what you do about them. The goal is to respond in a healthy way that allows you to feel content with the outcome of the situation and content that you have done the best you can within your abilities and options. Again, this may be something you need to work through using the techniques mentioned above.

Ultimately, when you allow yourself to process your emotions in an empowering way, you can begin to exude an attitude of peace, confidence, and contentment. There is nothing more beautiful than a genuine smile!

Let's Reflect

For this this-or-that style activity, you'll need a pencil as well as a marker or pen, preferably of a different color (not black). First, examine each pair of words and use the pencil to circle which of the two you typically do. Then, switch to your marker, examine each pair of words, and circle which of the two you prefer to do. By the end, you'll be able to see two things at a glance: any disconnects between your preferences and your reality, and a guiding list of activities you should focus on doing more often!

shower

or

bath

full closet

or

capsule wardrobe

face mask

or

exfoliation

manicure

or

pedicure

two-step skincare routine

or

ten-step skincare routine

just a trim

or

a full haircut

trendy clothes

or

classic basics

colored hair

or

natural hair

journaling

or

calling a friend

athleisure
clothes
or
dressy
outfits

naked nails
or
painted nails

light
makeup
or
a full face of
makeup

trying new
products
or
sticking to
the usual

meditation
or
moving your
body

Are there any personal-appearance or self-presentation activities or categories that weren't included here that are meaningful to you? List them with pairs of items as done in the activity.

_____   _____   _____

_____   _____   _____

_____   _____   _____

_____   _____   _____

_____   _____   _____

_____   _____   _____

Let's Visualize

You've started thinking about how you mold and experience your personal appearance in your daily life already with the previous activity; now it's time to dig into how you'd like to express yourself in an ideal world. Answer the journaling questions here, taking time to really sit and imagine your responses.

When you're going to a special event, how do you take time to prepare beforehand? List out every detail of personal hygiene that would make you feel your absolute best.

_____

_____

_____

_____

_____

_____

_____

Which items from the above list would you like to incorporate into your life on a regular basis? What might this look like on an average day or week?

_____

_____

_____

_____

_____

_____

_____

_____

What's your "thing"—a specific activity related to appearance that makes you feel like you are truly yourself? Describe how you would feel if you began to prioritize your "thing."

_____

_____

_____

_____

_____

_____

_____

Is there some new type of service, product, or trend that you have been wanting to try? How might you feel if this became a regular part of your life?

_____

_____

_____

_____

_____

_____

_____

Let's Grow

Pick a day this week to get wedding-ready. Obviously, skip the gown and updo, but genuinely try to complete the steps that you'd normally take to get ready to feel your best for a big event. Consider all the little details you take the time to prepare in terms of self-care prior to a big event and really commit to enacting them.

The next day, the day after you went through the whole process and did yourself up as if for a wedding, answer the following questions.

How did you feel when you took the time to prioritize a full personal hygiene routine this week?

_____

_____

_____

_____

What setbacks did you encounter while attempting to enact this routine?

_____

_____

_____

_____

How can you incorporate some or all of these practices into your usual routine?

_____

_____

_____

_____

Over the course of the coming month, be intentional about your personal appearance. Each time you complete one of the items in the chart below, place a check in the box. To raise the stakes, consider planning an incentive to reward yourself if you check off every item. Go ahead, mama, get yourself a little treat!

Try a mindfulness meditation	Use lotion, a face mask, or your favorite small luxury	Wear a favorite outfit
Schedule your favorite service or do a DIY at-home service	Trim or paint your nails or get your nails done at a salon	Journal about an emotion you've been holding on to
Get wedding-ready for the day	Call a friend to talk through a situation you've been processing	Donate clothing that no longer makes you feel confident
Take a warm bath or shower without rushing	Toss beauty and hygiene products that are expired or not useful	Wash and style your hair your favorite way

5

Quiet Time

The Quest to Find Quiet in the Midst of Chaos

In a world of laughter and joy, yelling and whining, toys and music, talking and more talking, it's no secret that with children come many, many noises. When I first started considering the concept of quiet time, it felt like a unicorn: mystical, beautiful, enticing, and entirely fictional.

How in the world can we work through the big emotions, the noise of play, and all the other sounds of raising children to find peace? Yes, it sounds impossible, but I'm here to tell you it's not a thing of fantasy. Although it may take a quest for you to unearth the hidden gem of quiet time each day, you can find it, and once you do, it's absolutely glorious and life changing.

Some of the material in this chapter overlaps with the quiet alone times before bed that we discussed in chapter 3; some of this chapter also overlaps with concepts we'll cover later in chapter 7. As you've probably guessed by now, improving all aspects of our lives as mothers means taking a holistic approach, not siloing every need into a neat, discrete category.

"Our deepest wishes are whispers of our authentic self. We must learn to respect them. We must learn to listen."

—SARAH BAN BREATHNACH

The hardest part of parenting for me by far has been overstimulation. My kids are 21 months and 18 months apart, so when I say that I am writing this in the weeds, I am truly in the weeds. I wouldn't trade it for the world, and I recognize that I am beyond blessed, but wow, a four-year-old, a two-year-old, and a baby are a lot of stimulation day in and day out. Sometimes I also feel that I have raised the chattiest children in the history of the world. You too? Maybe we should introduce them!

I love my children's ideas and genuinely enjoy their presence. The silly things they come up with bring the biggest smile to my face, and I want to keep it that way, but I can't enjoy their bustling and noisy zest for life without making time for peaceful, restorative practices in my life as well. And I can't respond calmly or confidently to crises without those practices either.

Let's go on a little trip down memory lane. I'll never forget the day I set up the supplies to color Easter eggs with all three of my girls. I was mentally patting myself on the back because they were going to have a blast. All the eggs were boiled and cooled, the rainbow of dye was arched across the tableclothed counter, our white crayons were ready and waiting to draw, and my mindset was golden. I was ready for us to have some good old-fashioned fun. Boy, was I in for a surprise.

In a matter of thirty seconds, one child had thrown up a questionable pink liquid all over her play kitchen while shrieking, another had reached into a "number two" diaper and was proudly displaying the contents like a trophy to me, and my angelic little baby was screaming bloody murder with such intensity that I ended up with spit-up down my shirt. It was a ballad of bodily fluids, and, as the conductor of this orchestra, I did not know where to turn first. What on earth do you do in the face of that?

Over time, I have realized that without quiet time, constant overstimulation turns me into a grouchy, short-tempered version of myself who struggles to handle the messy situations like these that inevitably arise in the world of parenting. We've heard it time and again, and it's true: you cannot pour from an empty cup. When my kids are having a hard time, I am always more patient, more calm, and better at problem-solving if I'm clear and mentally rested. The opposite is true when I haven't had the time to properly recharge. When I'm depleted and normal childhood experiences happen, like a fight over sharing or a meltdown when someone doesn't get their way, I struggle to respond in a way that makes me proud. Feelings of frustration and anger threaten to overtake me, which makes it nearly impossible for me to help my kids work through their own big emotions. The antidote to this overwhelm is downtime. When we allow our system to fully relax in a

As mothers, we need to be realistic about our needs not only before chaos ensues but also following a difficult scene.

setting devoid of noise and chaos, we can diffuse the pent-up feelings that threaten to push us to a heightened emotional state. We can better model and respond to the many emotions our kids face when our own mental well-being is nurtured.

Let's return to that chaotic Easter scene now. Once I realized that everyone was actually okay—just covered in varying levels of gross—I laughed. I mean, how absurd that all three kids would melt down in entirely different ways at the very same moment! It was a sitcom. I got everyone cleaned up and settled, placed the eggs back into the fridge, and made the executive decision that we all needed some good old-fashioned decompression time. I was proud of the way I triaged the trauma in that scenario, but I wasn't going to

push it with the potential of a spilled cup of food dye. As mothers, we need to be realistic about our needs not only before chaos ensues but also following a difficult scene. There was a time in my life when I would have pressed on inflexibly with the plan to color the eggs. I wish I were kidding, but I would genuinely set myself up for feelings of overwhelm through stubbornly refusing to deviate from my original plan. But sometimes we need to stray from what we thought the day would look like and be more attuned to our needs and our children's needs. Otherwise, we run the risk of setting ourselves up for failure.

After diving deep and reflecting on overstimulation and overwhelm, I was able to recognize that spreading myself too thin and ignoring my mind's call for peace and quiet was a recipe for disaster—and this applies to you too. Yeah, my Easter egg situation sucked. It was gross and hard, and, honestly, I couldn't have done much to prevent the way everything unraveled. But I made it through in a way that made me proud. I cleaned the girls up and got them settled on the couch (on top of a blanket with a bucket ready to catch any more half-digested breakfast), and I sat down to feed the baby. Everyone was quiet except Daniel Tiger on the TV. And, let me tell you, I did not feel an ounce of mom guilt over that screen time, because I knew I deserved it after that cleanup and I knew that my babies needed the rest.

Sometimes, like in my story, quiet time comes when our kids are sitting right next to us. After our egg-coloring drama, I cracked open my Kindle on the couch and took advantage of the fleeting peace. Yes, I was reading while breastfeeding, but this little multitasking moment brought me such tranquility. We can't always walk away and be alone. Would I have thoroughly enjoyed snuggling up with my cozy blanket and a book while sipping a warm mug of coffee overlooking the breezy trees through the window? Absolutely—but that's not always in the cards. Rather than wallowing in the idea of what could be but isn't, you must choose the route of taking the time where you can get it, even in modified form. Consider the expectations you have for your quiet time, and get rid of the mentality that it only counts when you're entirely alone. Why give up on so many potential moments of peace just because your kids are still in the room?

Of course, it took me a long time to get to this point. The process hasn't been all rainbows and butterflies. I was able to keep my cool in that situation

Consider the expectations you have for your quiet time, and get rid of the mentality that it only counts when you're entirely alone.

because of all of the hard work I had done creating meaningful recharge and reset time prior to that experience. But, as hard as it is to admit, there had been many times before then that I had found myself losing control of my emotions. My frustration, anger, and poor-me attitude would creep in and overcome my ability to think straight. I attribute these feelings of loss of control to the fact that I was not meeting my needs on a regular basis. The lack of time to recharge and feel like myself in the midst of big demands was directly impacting my mental state and my reactions to my kids' choices. I was slowly becoming a yeller. Whenever I would yell, in the moment, the release of emotion felt oddly good. I wanted to scream, so it felt good to scream. At least, it felt good for a few seconds, until the guilt and spiraling thoughts settled in, reminding me that this was not who I wanted to be to my kids. I aspired to form a loving bond with them that centered on understanding, empathy, and kindness; yelling at them was doing the exact opposite.

So, I dug deep to find out what was leading to my outbursts and how I could better react to my children's choices, which were sometimes less than desirable. This is when I concluded that I was feeling overwhelmed by the demands of being a mom. (Shocker, I know!) This was not my kids' fault and it was not my fault, but wallowing in the feeling made it my problem, and a huge problem at that. Unfortunately,

these feelings were leading to a direct impatience toward my kids, and that just didn't feel fair. After all, they're just trying to navigate life with the limited knowledge and experiences that they have, and they're looking to me to guide them. This also wasn't fair to me, because although I am their guide, I still am a living, breathing human with needs and am also trying to navigate life with the limited knowledge and experiences that *I* have.

Recognizing this forced me to figure out pockets of quiet time in which I could decompress and reflect on my emotions and reactions. I started journaling daily and came to some important realizations about decompression that I want to share with you in the following pages. I'll summarize them in broad strokes first, then we'll dive into each in detail as we continue:

Not all quiet time is created equal.

There is pure alone time, there is quiet time with the kids, there are short moments, and there are long hours. You have to learn to take advantage of all of it to maximize the rest and restoration you can get from a single day or week.

Not all quiet time activities are created equal.

Mind-numbing activities have their time and place, but they should fill up only a small fraction of your total quiet time.

Life with kids isn't always picture-perfect, and sometimes we have to carve out the time in a realistic way.

Let's unpack the first realization first: that not all quiet time is created equal and that you should seek out all types. There are typically a few pockets of quiet time throughout any parent's day; this might include early morning before the kids wake up, late at night after they go to bed, and moments while one or more kids are awake but at least one is napping or at preschool. Ideally, quiet time happens when you are totally alone, but as I mentioned earlier, life with kids isn't always picture-perfect, and sometimes we have to carve out the time in a realistic way.

Let's dive into the early-morning wake-up-before-the-kids time slot. For some people, this is a fantastic way to kickstart the day with either a workout, hot coffee, journaling, or reading. This sets the individual up for a successful day, and they already feel they knocked off some to-dos or found peace before the chaos. It is a fantastic opportunity for restorative alone time . . . unless your kids wake up at the crack of dawn. I've spoken to friends that would need to wake up at 4:00 a.m. to get morning

alone time! 4:00 a.m. is a no-go for me, as I am sure it is for many of you, and honestly I draw the line even at 6:00 a.m. There was a glorious time in my life when the girls slept in until 8:00 or 8:30 a.m., and then, sadly, as most good things do, that came to an end. I was so upset to have lost this morning quiet time when they began to throttle me awake much earlier than expected!

If an early wake-up works for you, seize it. What an amazing pocket of time to take advantage of! But if it does not work for you, then let it go. No two people or families are the same, and this is not one size fits all. And don't beat yourself up for sleeping a little longer in the morning, for catching up on your sleep debt when you can.

So if the morning won't work for you, we need to look for another pocket of time! The after-the-kids-go-to-bed quiet time is another great option when used appropriately. If you haven't already read chapter 3 and what it has to say about rest and the quiet hour before sleeping, what are you doing? Go back and review that chapter!

Now let's turn to quiet time while our kids are awake, because I know some of you are already rolling your eyes and thinking I am making it up altogether. I swear I'm not! There is simply no way I could have written this entire book in a year and read more than 100 books every year since my first daughter was born by simply using an hour or two at night for reading and writing. I'm going to explain an average day in our household now for you, so you can see where I personally sneak in quiet time.

First thing in the morning, I create quiet time to read while I'm nursing my youngest daughter. Sometimes I hold a physical book and really test my wrist strength, but most days I use my Kindle with a PopSocket on the back for ease. (If you're a reader—and you're here, so you're probably a reader—I highly recommend you try the PopSocket trick!) While I'm reading and feeding baby, my four-year-old and two-year-old are allowed to watch one or two episodes of a show that they agree on from PBS Kids or Vooks. (I love both options because they are educational yet entertaining. It took a bit of time and effort to wean them off the jam-packed action shows they were used to, but I genuinely see a difference in their behavior with these slower-paced options.) Often, if they're watching a show, I prefer to listen to a podcast or an audiobook to simultaneously engage in something that interests me and to block out the sound of their show.

A Word about Screen Time

I am slowly working toward weaning my kids off the morning shows, but it's a work in progress, and right now I choose to use this "tool" in the morning so I can peacefully nurse the baby. Some days, I set out blocks or coloring supplies and wait to see if they notice or care that the TV screen is black. I have been so pleasantly surprised by how often it doesn't even register in them that they aren't watching something. Again, it's a work in progress, and I am also a work in progress with my relationship to screens. Screen time is a mom-guilt trigger for me, and I'm giving myself grace as I figure it out. A trap that we as parents often fall into is an all-or-nothing mindset. It's okay to use tools, such as a tablet or a show; it only becomes a problem when it becomes a problem. So, in my daily morning practice with my girls, I try out quiet-time activities first and feel no guilt in saying yes to a morning TV show if they ask.

The second pocket of quiet time I have regularly is the time when my middle daughter and youngest daughter are simultaneously napping. This doesn't happen every day, but when it does, I take full advantage. This has grown into a ritual with my oldest daughter; we refer to it as journal time. I grab my journal or computer and she grabs her coloring book and crayons, and we work side by side. Some days she is very chatty, but it's been a great way to teach her patience. When we first started doing journal time together, it took a lot of scaffolding to get to the point where she wasn't interrupting every twenty or thirty seconds, so if you're attempting to form a quiet-time ritual with your child or children, remember that it won't happen overnight. You will have to slowly

work your way up toward larger and increasingly peaceful pockets of time.

Okay, enough about our kids—there's one more category of quiet time you might be able to plumb. I'm talking about quiet time outside the house, free of the kids, during the day! If you work outside the home, maybe your lunch break can be your quiet time. When I worked as a teacher, I loved using my lunch break to read a book. Sure, chitchatting in the lounge was appealing, and some days my mind called for that, but other days I loved the comfort of reading in silence. I craved that time during work to avoid feeling overstimulated in the same way I crave the silence as a stay-at-home mom. I'm embarrassed to admit how long it took me to

If you're attempting to form a quiet-time ritual with your children, remember that it won't happen overnight.

Be open to getting creative with your time.

recognize the parallels of my needs for decompression in the classroom setting and the home setting. I should have been taking advantage of the pockets of quiet in the same way I did when I was teaching, but my brain was instead fixated on doing *more, more, more* while my girls were sleeping. Once the Aha! moment happened, I never turned back. The girls were going to witness me working in the same way I would let my students witness me grading their papers and exams: when they worked, I worked. We appreciated each other's focus and energy when we could see them in action.

Another way you could take advantage of quiet time while working at a traditional full-time job can be during your commute. I started listening to podcasts and audiobooks on mine, which made me look forward to the

drive rather than dreading it. I was able to utilize otherwise "unproductive" time spent driving to tap into hobbies I loved. Now, I listen to a book or podcast while I fold the laundry. It's calming and makes the chore feel less tedious. Each time you discover pockets of personal time like these throughout the day, you give yourself the opportunity to move from a fixed mindset to a growth mindset. Be open to getting creative with your time—you'll start to recognize that a few minutes here and there can morph into an hour or more. The metaphorical branches begin to extend and grow. A mindset that once told you "you have no time for that" will begin to uncover the spaces where you do in fact have time.

If you've read this far, you've certainly got plenty of ideas for when and how to find or make quiet time for yourself

Looking into where you can make quiet time and how best to spend it can take you from a constant feeling of "I never get time to myself" to "I found time for myself."

throughout the day. Now let's return to the second big realization I wanted to discuss: that not all quiet-time activities are created equal.

Imagine this scenario that you've probably experienced countless times already: the kids have fought bedtime so hard that you simply collapse onto the couch in defeat and pray that there aren't any further requests for another sip of water, a visit to the bathroom, extra kisses or hugs, or any other stalling tactic under the sun. (The world says we will miss this when they're older, and I don't doubt that for one second, because it is so genuinely sweet that our babies want just one more minute of time with us each night, but it's still entirely exhausting to go through the rigamarole of bedtime every evening!) On days like these, we might simply collapse moments after

we shut their bedroom door, and we often don't feel like we have the energy for any quality quiet time.

This danger zone of mental and physical exhaustion can lead to something I have referred to previously as mindless or mind-numbing activities; we discussed this at length in chapter 3. We are so exhausted that we simply can't think anymore, so we scroll on social media, zone out on Netflix, shovel snacks into our mouths, or crack open a bottle of wine. I'm not saying these are inherently bad things to do, and I've done my fair share, but these actions are not usually what leaves us feeling fulfilled, especially if they are what we turn to on a regular basis. Rather than leaving us feeling refreshed and reenergized, they often leave us feeling further depleted and craving even more downtime. This is not a sustainable use of quiet time—this is succumbing to mindlessness.

I switched from scrolling on social media at night to reading a book, which is a hobby that I've always enjoyed. I downloaded an app to remind me to ignore my phone (counterintuitive, yes, but it helped!). As hard as it was, I worked to break the habit of numbing my brain before bedtime. Time spent on our phone isn't inherently bad, and catching up with friends can be so easy through social media or texting, but it is a slippery slope. Time on our phones can shift quickly from a couple of minutes to a couple of hours. I fall back into the trap occasionally and have to hop back on the wagon; I

remind myself that this is my pocket of daily recharge time, and I need to take advantage of it so I can head into the next day feeling energized and fresh.

All right, we have covered a lot of ground in this chapter, and I'm sure you have a lot to think about! Truly, forming new habits and looking into where you can make quiet time and how best to spend it can take you from a constant feeling of "I never get time to myself" to "I found time for myself." This deep prioritization of self will help you to decompress, regulate your emotions, and encourage your unique sense of self outside the many roles you balance.

Let's Reflect

Answer the following questions in the space provided. Really consider what the answers would look like for you in your current life, not just how the world or social media defines these ideas. We can't wave a magic wand to achieve perfect amounts of quiet time, but we can genuinely consider our daily lives to uncover little pockets of time that may already exist, and use those moments in meaningful ways.

How do you define quiet time?

_____

_____

_____

List a few ways that quiet time could be useful for you to rest and restore.

_____

_____

_____

List a few ways that quiet time could be useful for you to find fulfillment.

_____

_____

_____

What is your reaction to the idea of quiet time *with* your children? How about *without* your children?

_____

_____

_____

List a few pockets of your day where you could find five or ten minutes of quiet.

_____

_____

_____

What quiet-time activities would you like to do within your home? How about outside your home?

_____

_____

_____

What is your reaction to the idea of morning quiet time? Evening quiet time?

_____

_____

_____

Brainstorm a few ideas for your kids to do while you are having quiet time.

_____

_____

_____

Describe the space where you would want to be for your at-home quiet time.

_____

_____

_____

Let's Visualize

Consider what your ideal vision for quiet time would look like practically in a day, a week, and a month. Once you have spent a few moments considering this, answer the questions below.

How would you like to find quiet in the day-to-day?

_____

_____

_____

On a weekly basis, what would quiet time look like for you?

_____

_____

_____

Throughout an entire month, which items would be "musts" on your list of quiet-time activities?

_____

_____

_____

Now that you have taken the time to get clear about what you'd like to use your time for, try the following two tasks this week:

Find one time this week to have quiet time with your child(ren) around.

Find one time this week to have quiet time without your child(ren) around.

Then return to the prompts on the facing page to evaluate how you feel about your progress!

How did your quiet time with children go?

_____

_____

What roadblocks did you hit? What modifications can you make so things run more smoothly?

_____

_____

Was the task or activity you chose to do during this time suitable for having your child(ren) nearby? If not, what is a more suitable choice?

_____

_____

How did your quiet time without children go? Explain how you felt emotionally and physically afterward.

_____

_____

What roadblocks did you hit? What modifications can you make to fully and wisely use this time?

_____

_____

What other tasks or activities would you like to try during this time?

_____

_____

Let's Grow

For an entire week, choose one time each day to have at least ten minutes (more is great) of quiet time. Record your results in the chart on this page. Then make necessary modifications and try it again the following week.

WEEK 1	Where and when did you find quiet time? How did you use it?	Would you do this again?
Monday		
Tuesday		
Wednesday		
Thursday		
Friday		
Saturday		
Sunday		

WEEK 2	Where and when did you find quiet time? How did you use it?	Would you do this again?
Monday		
Tuesday		
Wednesday		
Thursday		
Friday		
Saturday		
Sunday		

6

Let's Get Moving

Intentional Movement as a Source of Power and Pride

As parents, especially parents of young children, it's easy to think that chasing our kids around is enough movement in a day. It's true that this can be exhausting, but I still genuinely believe we should also make moving our bodies with some form of intentional exercise a priority.

When we take the time to exercise, not only does our body benefit but also our mind and mood. It's no secret that exercise releases the feel-good endorphins that help fight stress and fatigue, and that's crucial in a parent's day-to-day life.

Sometimes, the hardest part about forming a workout routine is just showing up. We make excuses or put it off for tomorrow, until one day we look back and realize that our exercise has fallen off entirely. You are probably familiar with the urge to skip your workout, but you also probably know how glad you are to have stuck to it once you're done.

"Fitness is an entry point to help you build that happier, healthier life. When your health is strong, you're capable of taking risks. You'll feel more deserving of love."

—JILLIAN MICHAELS

When you form a realistic plan to intentionally move your body on a regular basis and commit to showing up and giving it your all, you'll begin to see the myriad of benefits. It'll begin to feel not only manageable but also like a nonnegotiable. There's just no denying the strength and mental clarity that comes from taking care of your physical body through movement, and once you embrace that, it'll be hard to turn back. In the following pages, we'll work through several key aspects of incorporating movement into your daily life as a mom:

The importance of active recovery

Working with your menstrual cycle

How to get and stay motivated

How to practically find time
for exercise

The importance of
accountability partners

As we move forward, it's important to note that not every day will look the same and that you won't always be working at top-tier output. If you make a habit of pushing yourself to your max every single workout, you'll likely run yourself ragged and wind up with an injury or a feeling of burnout that leads to taking time off from working out, sometimes for months on end. You also have to be careful not to swing too far

in the opposite direction: it's vital to make sure that your workouts are not so laid-back that you don't experience the benefits of active movement.

Personally, I struggle with becoming fixated on working out for weeks and weeks until I inevitably burn out because my body is tired and I feel I "deserve" a rest. Of course I deserve a rest—we all do—but the type of rest you will actually benefit from is very different from the type of rest that involves eating potato chips on the couch for two weeks straight until you finally crave movement again.

This is where the concept of active recovery comes in. Active recovery is a broad term that means low-impact or gentle exercises that can be done as part of your workout, between two workouts, or on rest days between more-strenuous workout days; it allows your body to process the benefits of exercise while discouraging fatigue.

Active recovery has become an integral part of my relationship with exercising, and I highly recommend you integrate it too. On rest days and between focused workouts, you can maintain the habit of movement, but incorporate gentle low-impact exercises like stretching, walking, yoga, and cycling to give your body the rest it needs. These don't have to be long sessions—even 20 or 30 minutes can give benefits. Embracing a practice of active recovery has been a game changer for me; now, I experience much less exercise

As females, our menstrual cycle can have a huge impact on how a month plays out, but we don't have to be victims of our cycles.

burnout, and, since my body has ample time to recover, I can approach more-challenging workouts with more vigor than I did in the past. Frankly, I am stronger, have more energy, and see physical changes in my body.

Another area that I recommend you factor into your plan for physical health is the concept of cycle-syncing your workouts. As females, our menstrual cycle can have a huge impact on how a month plays out, but we don't have to be victims of our cycles. This is not to say that at times—or maybe even all the time—our periods don't stop us in our tracks with pain and discomfort. It is to say that we can use our knowledge of the seasons of our cycle to empower ourselves.

In brief, our cycle can be characterized by the four seasons: winter (menstruation), spring (follicular phase),

summer (ovulation), and fall (luteal phase). In many women, these phases come with different energy levels, which is where the seasons metaphor comes in. When you consider the movement of your body within these phases, think of generally how you might feel in each of the seasons associated with that phase. For example, in the winter, you may feel the urge to slow down and rest. The menstruation phase is indeed typically our lowest-energy phase of the four. Do not deny your body this rest time! I like to think of my movement during menstruation as a form of gentle self-care to restore my body and prepare for the following seasons. I might opt for a deep and restful yoga practice with an emphasis on stretching and mindful awareness rather than an intense hot-yoga flow. This is especially true on day one of my cycle. For me, these gentle movements help my body recover from higher-intensity workouts while keeping the habit of movement alive.

As you move into the follicular phase of your cycle, you will probably start to feel an increase in your energy and strength. For me, this often means I crave a workout! I want to hit my personal records on the cycling bike or try a new weightlifting technique. I feel up to the challenge! And now that I'm aware of this information—now that I understand that I typically feel this way during the follicular phase—I know that I can lean into this natural change and intensify my workouts through both spring and summer (ovulation). For most women, ovulation is the phase at which you'll hit peak energy.

Once fall—the luteal phase—approaches, many women will notice their energy starting to dip a little. Rather than beating yourself up over this shift, you can recognize what your body is telling you: start to slow down and give yourself ample recovery time. Taper your way down into winter again.

Listening to your cycle and honoring what your body needs throughout the month can be such a positive experience. I highly recommend trying this method to increase the productivity of your workouts, capitalize on rest and recovery, diversify your movement types, and gain an all-around better respect and understanding of the inner workings of your body.

Of course, your menstrual cycle and your relationship with your own body are both highly personal. When you think about exercise and movement, your thoughts might be quite different from your neighbor, friend, family member, or any other mom that you come across throughout your life. Don't

When my daughters think of strength, I don't want them to assume that it's a characteristic meant only for boys and men; I want to raise strong and powerful girls.

fib to yourself about your lived reality in an effort to adhere to what is typical. That said, it can be very beneficial to find a sense of camaraderie with other women in your journey toward a healthier exercise lifestyle.

Now let's turn our attention toward how to get and stay motivated. If you find yourself having a difficult time staying motivated to work out consistently throughout the month, start by evaluating your "why." Get past the initial thoughts of "Well, I know I should" and seek a genuine answer. For me, I love how working out makes me feel strong. I crave the rush I get from running just a little farther than the last time and the power I feel when I can lift a little more this session. Another big motivating factor for me is how my body and mind feel when I am consistently dedicating time to working out: I feel strong, proud, and mentally clear. Wrapped up in these personal reasons is another huge factor: I am obsessed with modeling good behavior for my girls. I want my daughters to see me taking care of myself. When they think of strength, I don't want

them to assume that it's a characteristic meant only for boys and men; I want to raise strong and powerful girls. Once I consciously acknowledged all these "whys" for myself, I found it easier to drum up the motivation to start workouts as well as the motivation to give them my all.

I think by now you understand that committing to exercise is not easy, but that it is absolutely worth it. Now that we have considered our why and talked about motivation, we also need to determine the how, because one of the factors that I hear most often cited by moms struggling to establish an exercise routine is "I don't have time."

We are busy, undoubtedly. We all work to juggle the many demands of life—raising children, housework, jobs, obligations, duties; the list goes on. The question is, should we use these as an excuse to put our health on the back burner? This may be a hard truth to hear, but we prioritize what we *want* to prioritize. In simpler terms, when you say yes to one thing, you are often saying no to something else. So let's make sure we say yes to good health practices.

Over the course of my time as a mom, I've used trial and error to figure out the best way to fit exercising into my daily life. I had to consider my options and decide what was realistic for me. For a long while, I felt the pressure to wake up earlier than my kids so I could squeeze in a workout before they woke up, but that pressure wasn't enough for me to make a permanent shift. Instead, I just felt guilty for not waking up in time, resentful that my kids were waking up early enough that I felt I couldn't wake up in time, and like a failure because so many moms do successfully wake up in time! The point is, I am not a morning person, and this plan was just not going to work for me.

In some alternate life, maybe I'll be up exercising at 4:00 a.m. so that I am showered and ready for the day with a mug of steaming coffee all before my children leap out of their beds. That would be such a beautiful experience, but, ultimately, being asleep in my bed at 4:00 a.m. is more appealing to me, so I knew I needed to explore other options.

The next avenue I decided to explore was working out while one or more of my kids was awake. This worked well when I had one or two kids. With one kid in the picture, most of the time I could squeeze in a half hour or so of exercise with only minor interruptions. Alas, the seasons shifted, as did the needs of my children. With the introduction of potty training, it became

When you say yes to one thing, you are often saying no to something else.

It was too easy to fall into the trap of the "I'm so tired" narrative.

hard to really get into a workout when I was regularly at risk of needing to stop and sprint a toddler to the toilet every few minutes.

This is when my husband and I decided to start doing family workouts. Okay, it sounds corny, but stick with me here. Basically, this just means that the whole family goes downstairs to the unfinished portion of our basement where our workout equipment is, and my husband and I both work out at the same time while the kids amuse themselves nearby. We installed temporary net fencing to separate the equipment from the kids' side of the basement for safety. This gives us peace of mind that no one will get hurt while also giving us the chance to have help from one another when either of us is doing a workout that is hard to start

and stop (like clipping in and out of the Peloton bike, sprinting on the treadmill, or using heavy weights).

Part of the reason that family workouts have worked out so well for me is that my husband has become my accountability partner. But I want to rewind here for a second, because the story of how I got here was not so simple and easy!

As I became a mom to more and more children, it was still proving really difficult for me to stick to working out consistently. It was too easy to fall into the trap of the "I'm so tired" narrative. There was a period of time when I would watch my husband go to work out in the basement while I stayed on the couch because I simply didn't want to join him. Sure, I'd feel a little guilty

Although exercise is individual to your body, you do not have to go it alone.

about it, but that wasn't enough to create a lasting change in me . . . yet. So, I decided to tap into a resource that had become invaluable in my life: the Bookstagram community.

What's Bookstagram and what the heck does it have to do with workouts, you ask? Bookstagram is a book-obsessed section of Instagram. Seriously, obsessed. We all share pictures of books, reviews of books, tips on how to read more books, books we love, books we don't love, recommendations, where to buy your books, what book gadgets to buy—you get the point. The thing about the traditional format of reading (which involves a physical book in your hand) is that, unless you're Belle from *Beauty and the Beast* and you have mastered reading, singing, and casually strolling through the town as everyone watches, you kind of have to

sit down to read. And, I realized, a lot of readers on Bookstagram also really want to try to include more physical movement into their days.

So, over the past few years, I decided to run a free monthly challenge via my Bookstagram account to motivate people to get their bodies moving (and to make time for reading; most were already reading a ton, though, so this was just a unifying factor). Through hosting this monthly challenge and the accompanying motivational chat groups, I've witnessed the life-changing impact of working out and moving intentionally in hundreds of women. I have also been highly motivated as the host. The impact is astounding. Not only do we feel more energetic, stronger, and healthier because we engaged in these challenges to care for our bodies physically, but most of us also feel more patient and present with our family, sleep better at night, and experience less stress and anxiety.

As I mentioned, my husband's workouts weren't enough to motivate me to really dedicate my time and energy to consistently exercising. However, the combination of my Bookstagram accountability groups and our family workouts has managed to solidify my daily habit of movement. When my husband gets home from work, we set a time for when we are going to go work out that evening, and we stick to it. This has now become a daily habit and second nature, even if the exact time fluctuates.

Having a built-in accountability partner has been so helpful. If your spouse or partner can be your accountability partner, fantastic! It's convenient because you most likely live together and maybe are on somewhat similar schedules. If you are single or your spouse won't work as an accountability partner for any reason, your accountability partner could be a friend or different family member instead.

If you have the opportunity, another great way to find motivation while holding yourself accountable is through group fitness classes or in-gym classes. For a while, this didn't seem doable for me. I had to arrange childcare and contort my schedule to make it work, but for the better part of the last two years, I have been going to my yoga studio once a week for an in-person yoga class. Every so often, this matches up with my friends' schedule and we get to practice together, which is a beautiful thing! I've also begun to meet people in the studio, so the sessions do double duty, giving me the movement I need as well as a chance for positive social interactions with other adults. Win, win!

If a group class or in-gym workout doesn't seem realistic to your life, consider free options like walking, hiking, running, or buddy workouts at your house, a friend's house, or a local park. I love when movement can coincide with social interactions. When I was in college, my roommates and I would often walk to the gym together to work out—I didn't realize it at the time, but we had chosen one another as our accountability partners. It's true that as adults living in different homes, it takes a little more coordination to set this up, but think creatively here. You can call each other on the drive to the gym, choose the same Peloton class or YouTube video to simultaneously do from each of your homes, have weekly check-ins on progress and goals . . . the options are endless! Although exercise is individual to your body, you do not have to go it alone.

I hope that I've given you plenty to think about regarding establishing an exercise practice that works for your body and your lifestyle. Let's dive into the activities and start putting it all into action!

Let's Reflect

To get started, let's appraise what exercise looks like in your life right now. Check always, sometimes, or never for each prompt. This exercise works best when you are wholly honest, so don't hold back. It also helps to consider these prompts generally throughout the course of a week or month as you respond, rather than pinned to a specific day.

ALWAYS	SOMETIMES	NEVER	
○	○	○	I feel good about my workout routine on a weekly basis.
○	○	○	My body feels strong and healthy.
○	○	○	I feel motivated to move my body daily.
○	○	○	My workouts are often indoors.
○	○	○	My workouts are often outdoors.
○	○	○	I have the strength and energy to play with my kids.
○	○	○	I feel motivated to try new workouts.
○	○	○	My feelings about exercising are positive.
○	○	○	I work out with a friend or partner.
○	○	○	I work out solo.
○	○	○	I exercise when my kids are nearby.
○	○	○	I attend in-person workout classes.
○	○	○	I go to a workout facility outside my home.
○	○	○	My movement routine includes days for active recovery.
○	○	○	I am highly motivated to exercise on a regular basis.
○	○	○	My workouts are challenging but attainable.
○	○	○	I stay engaged in my workouts rather than just going through the motions.
○	○	○	If I find a good routine, I can stick to it.

Let's Visualize

Now that we've taken the time to reflect on your current patterns of exercise, let's identify your motivations and goals. Figuring out your "why" is the most crucial piece of this puzzle. When you have a solid reason for prioritizing exercise, it's much easier to stay motivated and to say yes to your workouts even when your mind is urging you to skip them. Once you ingrain your why in your mind, you can work to visualize a movement plan that fits into your life.

Consider what your life will look like when you have a regular movement plan in place. How do you feel physically, emotionally, and mentally?

_____

_____

_____

_____

_____

_____

_____

Who or what is your why? This is your reason and main motivation for prioritizing exercise on a regular basis. When you get stuck, your why should be able to help you push forward.

_____

_____

_____

_____

_____

_____

_____

Who can help support you on your journey toward your exercise goals? Think of this person (or people) as your accountability partner. How will you connect with your accountability partner?

_____

_____

_____

_____

_____

Brainstorm a plan for what an average day will look like for you in terms of exercise. Do you plan to exercise indoors or outdoors? At what time of day? With your children or without them? How will your accountability partner show up (text, call, meet up)?

_____

_____

_____

_____

_____

_____

What workouts have you been interested in trying out? Consider in-person options as well as virtual options. Remember that not every workout has to involve a traditional gym or expensive equipment—a habit of taking a hike in the park can be just as beneficial as a pricey monthly membership.

_____

_____

_____

_____

_____

Don't forget to consider active recovery as part of your exercise routine. Giving our body adequate rest while sticking to our movement habits can be beneficial in staying motivated and keeping ourselves safe and healthy. What active-recovery options are on your list to try out?

_____

_____

_____

_____

_____

After taking the time to answer all the above questions, plan out a week of movement in the chart below. Then execute it!

	Activity and Time	How did it go? Would you do this again?
Monday		
Tuesday		
Wednesday		
Thursday		
Friday		
Saturday		
Sunday		

Let's Grow

The idea of transitioning from 20–30 minutes of exercise per day for zero days a week to seven days a week can be daunting. If you bite off more than you can chew, you may end up burning out or giving up because the goal is too far beyond the scope of your current practice. Determine a consistent day, time, and place for your workouts and focus on showing up for just a few minutes of exercise each time for the course of a month. Once you build up the habit of arriving, you'll begin to see your exercise time extend.

As you embark on this journey, it's also important to figure out what activities you actually enjoy doing. The more enjoyable an activity is, the more likely you'll be to stick with it. This month, try out a bunch of the activity ideas provided. Use the number scale to indicate how you felt about each activity after completing it.

Do not feel pressured to complete every single box in one month! You can revisit these pages down the line as you continue to try out new activities each month.

1	**2**	**3**	**4**
I loved it and would do it again! I want to make this a regular part of my life.	I enjoyed this and could see myself doing it a few times per week.	This somewhat worked for me, but I could only see doing it occasionally.	This didn't really fit into my plan or goals for the future.

I tried out an in-person workout class focused on

_____

I tried out an online workout class focused on

_____

I tried out active recovery in the form of yoga.

I tried out active recovery in the form of stretching or foam rolling.

I tried out active recovery in the form of walking.

I tried out active recovery in the form of _____

I tried _____ as an outdoor workout.

I tried _____ as an indoor workout.

I tried a weightlifting workout.

I tried a cardio workout.

I tried a cycling or spinning workout.

I tried a swimming or water-based workout.

I tried having an accountability partner: _____

I tried a workout with my kids nearby.

I tried a workout without my kids nearby.

7

Personal Fulfillment

Embracing Your Unique Identity and What Fulfills You

At the end of the day, we are all unique, and our personal and mental needs vary just as much as our personalities, preferences, and identities. These traits may even vary throughout our lives.

As mothers, it's natural to feel that a huge chunk of your identity is wrapped up in mothering. I always say that being a mom is one of my favorite aspects of my identity, but we can't stop there.

If you continually direct all your mental energy exclusively toward the care of your children, you'll lose out on the journey of discovering the other beautiful aspects of your own identity. Imagine if you encouraged and celebrated all the wonderful parts of yourself in the same way that you did for your children. It's life-changing to recognize what makes you feel alive and to reach for it!

In this chapter, it's time to focus on what makes you *you* and how to allow your unique self to flourish.

"Success, I would find out, is interior. It has to do with self-fulfillment and the joy of living."

—SOPHIA LOREN

When you live in authenticity and prioritize the things that make you you, your life begins to take on a different shape. You can still complete the tedious, mundane, or stressful tasks needed to keep things running smoothly, but you'll have a greater purpose beyond the to-dos. You will feel a deep sense of connection to yourself.

When I first became a mom, I decided to step away from my career as a middle-school teacher. I knew that the door to teaching might not be forever closed, but I felt the call to stay home with my baby for the near future. Upon starting my role as a stay-at-home mom rather than an educator, I could tell that something was missing, and it took some soul-searching to figure out what that was. It wasn't necessarily my job itself or the sense of pride and security that came with earning an income, though those were great in their own ways. Rather, for me, it was mostly about creativity. I realized that a lot of my identity was wrapped up in the creativity of being a teacher. As an English and reading teacher, I found a sense of accomplishment, pride, and joy in planning and implementing fun, interactive lessons. I also loved creating my own resources and watching my students have Aha! moments in the classroom. Although I willingly and excitedly decided to stay at home versus returning to the classroom, as time progressed, I knew I needed to find ways to feel that creative energy again.

I brainstormed quite a lot in the service of figuring out how to get the creative fulfillment I so craved. As I pursued different opportunities and hobbies, I realized that some of the roles I had envisioned for myself weren't actually a good fit; in some cases, I had romanticized ideas in a "the grass is greener on the other side" way. Once I began to follow my heart, though, I was able to find a creative outlet that I felt passionate about. (More on that later!)

Whether you are working in a traditional job earning an income or staying home with your children, you still need to determine where you are meeting your need for a sense of personal and mental fulfillment in life. Maybe for you, this looks like focusing on the upbringing of your children and running an ideal home; maybe it looks like pursuing different hobbies and passions; or maybe it comes from your dedication to your career.

At the end of the day, you are responsible for meeting your personal needs for fulfillment; it will come from your daily choices. I want to emphasize this: *you* are responsible for whether or not you feel fulfilled mentally and personally. Now, in no way, shape, or form is this an easy thing to achieve, and it will look different for every person. Taking responsibility for your personal and mental needs could mean making a huge shift (such as

We are all wildly different and wonderfully unique.

changing jobs), opting for part-time work, budgeting for you to stay at home, or leaving the home to reenter the workforce. It could also mean continuing to do whatever you've been doing workwise but focusing on passions and hobbies separate from work that bring you joy. We can't all quit our jobs and take a solo trip around the globe to find ourselves—especially not with kids!—but we can sit with our emotions to uncover what provides a spark of light in our life and chase that energy. Whichever shift is needed will reveal itself to you. Trust your intuition. Remember too that comparing yourself to other moms is the fastest way to sabotage your own sense of identity. We are all wildly different and wonderfully unique.

For example, one of my closest friends loves to run half and full marathons, and gosh, she is an inspiration! As a former runner, I remember thinking for a moment, "Wow, should I run a marathon?" But the answer is no! The idea of doing that is painful to me at this point in my life, even though for her it's empowering and exhilarating. By letting go of the thought that you should also be pursuing the accomplishments that others value, you make space for two different things. First, you allow yourself to be wholly happy for your friends and loved ones and proud of their accomplishments without getting down on yourself or feeling envious. Second, you make space for yourself to find a path that gives you empowerment and joy in the same way others' goals do for them. There is no checklist for the "right" opportunities to pursue, but when you do follow the path that's right for you, then you'll feel the power of true alignment.

Personally, I had always dreamed of staying home with my children, so I was shocked that I was having all these feelings of discontent about the reality of being a stay-at-home mom. I wasn't prepared for the complicated feeling of wanting to be right where I was while also wondering why it felt like something was missing. After reaching out to my friends, I realized that this is a very common experience for stay-at-home moms. I wouldn't have chosen to be anywhere else, and I am eternally thankful for this opportunity, but I had

a nagging feeling that I wanted a little something more added to my current role—something that felt uniquely beneficial to *me*.

As I mentioned earlier in this chapter, I knew I needed to find a creative outlet that I felt passionate about. Here's where Bookstagram comes in! I decided to start my own Bookstagram account in September 2020, and it was a great personal decision. This social media account became a place for me to use my creative energy and to connect to other people who love reading. I found great joy in creating content, reviewing books, hosting group chats and book club discussions, and embracing my hobby fully. The

Don't feel as if fulfilling your personal
need is something that needs to happen
entirely within your own head . . .
don't hesitate to involve others!

best part was that it cost me zero dollars and I could partake in every facet directly from my home, which made it so achievable. And opening this account has since given back to me in many other ways, especially in terms of connection and community.

Once you figure out what outlet or activity will bring you personal fulfillment, you might be surprised at how many new doors it opens up and new self-discoveries it encourages. As you start spending time and energy on whatever hobby or pursuit fulfills you, I highly recommend that you look for a community aspect. This could be strictly through social media, or it could be in person; you could read through forum posts once a week or meet up with crafting buddies once a month— whatever makes sense for you. The point is, don't feel as if fulfilling your personal need is something that has to happen entirely within your own head or using just your own hands. Don't hesitate to involve others!

For me, shortly after joining the online Bookstagram community, I happened upon a local book club made up of other Bookstagrammers. We meet in person once a month to discuss books and life in general. Attending these meetings is such a fun way to meet my personal need for adult time. I look forward to these meaningful conversations and lasting connections with this set of new friends. (They have been endlessly supportive to me in my journey of writing this book as well.)

Joining Bookstagram also opened a second door for me: the owner of my local yoga studio approached me after following my account and offered me a position as the host for our yoga studio book club! I was absolutely over the moon when she called to chat about this opportunity. The sense of community, connection, accomplishment, and joy I receive from running this book club allows me to tap into the parts of teaching that I thought were lost to me. Both Bookstagram and the book club I host bring me fulfillment in different ways. You, too, can connect with the communities around your personal interests in many different ways.

Once you spend enough time, over the course of weeks and often months, dedicating yourself to things that you find personally fulfilling, you will likely discover that the self-value you derive or previously derived from work is not exclusive to work. The amazing things about yourself are inherent to *you*, not to something specific that you do. For me, this meant understanding that my traits of being driven, creative, social, and outgoing are not taken away from me simply because I no longer go to a workplace each day. This was a huge revelation for me, and I hope that you soon have a similar epiphany.

This is not to say that jobs can't be good sources of personal fulfillment, because of course they can! Sometimes a traditional job can give you an authentic connection to your identity.

This could be full time, part time, gig or freelance, long term, or short term. For a brief stint between the birth of my first and second daughters, I worked for Stitch Fix as a personal stylist. I loved this job! Not only was I able to have flexible hours and work from home, but I also reconnected with that creative energy I had missed so much by helping people find confidence and a sense of self via the clothing they wore each day. Frankly, it was fun!

However, as my maternity leave came to a close, I began to realize that it wouldn't be realistic to continue this work with two children in my care instead of just one. I had to make a hard decision: Do I continue to work and search for childcare? Or do I quit my job and act again as the sole childcare provider in my family? I chose to walk away from the job, and it felt right to me. I knew that that opportunity had served its purpose and believed that new potential would be right around the corner. Sometimes jobs, hobbies, and choices serve us for a time in a beautiful way, and we can walk away from them on a pleasant note to pursue future opportunities.

As you proceed on your journey of figuring out what fulfills you and how to make time for it in your life, be careful not to fall into the trap of thinking your needs are met when in reality you've just become numb to recognizing your own true identity apart from motherhood. It can be surprisingly easy to become caught up entirely in your role as a mother; before you know it, you may find yourself orbiting solely around your children. I've heard resigned admissions countless times from moms saying, essentially, "I wish I still did this or that, but the kids have (insert countless clubs, activities, sports, hobbies, etc.), and I love watching them pursue their passions!" But this does not have to be an all-or-nothing situation. Just because your kids have hobbies doesn't mean that you cannot. You have so many wonderful attributes that make you a beautifully complete person, and being a mom is indeed one part of that, but you have to make sure it's not the only part—otherwise, you will unwittingly sow the seeds of resentment.

Maybe you have already started down this path. Are you feeling overwhelmed and discouraged because you don't know who you are anymore? Are you unsure how you can feel like yourself when everyone needs you to show up 24/7 as "Mom"? These are clear signs that you might be feeling resentful in your role because of a lack of personal identity.

You need time in your life to fulfill roles other than "Mom." Let's look at an example. When I was a middle-school teacher (before I became a mom), the role meant that when I was working, I was a leader, an educator, a mentor, an authority figure, a guide, and more. On some days, when I would get into my car to go home, I'd take a deep breath, because being "on" all day was

You need time in your life to fulfill roles other than "Mom."

exhausting! I loved to decompress by phoning a friend on the drive home to chitchat about the previous night's episode of *The Bachelor*, or by meeting up with my boyfriend (now husband) for dinner at our favorite taco-and-margarita restaurant. Neither of these activities fit my role as a middle-school teacher, but they were important to my identity outside of my teacher role. Your identity is made up of many different interests, hobbies, dreams, roles, and characteristics. Just as I needed a little time off from middle-school teacher mode, you also will need time off from mom mode.

Have you ever stepped away from your role as a mom for a few hours and realized how freeing it is to be responsible for only yourself? Remember how rejuvenating it was to do what you alone wanted to do for that time? You felt that way because you have your own identity, and you were given a reminder of how much you appreciate the time to nurture that identity. We don't love our children less if we miss one soccer game to take a

pottery class we've been daydreaming about. Again, motherhood is not all or nothing. You are still a good mom if you let your child choose just one or two activities rather than five, so that you spend less time playing chauffeur and more time pursuing the dusty hobby box you left in the attic.

As mothers, we often prioritize the role of mom above everything else because we love our children and families, so we want to support them limitlessly! But you should not underestimate how truly valuable the time you spend nurturing your own identity is long term. This time recharges your soul and combats resentment, and you will model a healthy relationship with the self that is such a blessing for your children to see.

The process of figuring out what your unique personal and mental needs are—and, just as importantly, how you can take responsibility and action steps to meet those individual needs—requires a huge level of dedication. The path may not be easy, but the payout is life changing, I promise.

Let's Reflect

Discovering your identity is a dynamic, lifelong journey. As human beings, we change over the course of time, and new or different roles can shift our sense of self for better or worse. In order to live a life of happiness and fulfillment with confidence that we are embodying our genuine selves, we must be willing to sit with our thoughts, hopes, and dreams in a raw and honest way.

In the spaces below, jot down your responses to uncover some of the important aspects of your true identity. It's okay if you do not fill every single line in one sitting. Feel free to return to these boxes after considering the ideas over time. It's also okay if some of your responses include some negativity—we will work to uncover strategies for growth in the next section.

What three words describe your personality?

_____

_____

_____

What three roles do you play in life?

_____

_____

_____

What three hobbies or activities bring you joy?

_____

_____

_____

What three words describe you as a mother?

_____

_____

_____

What three items are barriers to being your best self?

_____

_____

_____

What three characteristics would you like to embody?

_____

_____

_____

What three actions would you like to add to your life?

_____

_____

_____

What three words would you like to be described as by others?

_____

_____

_____

Let's Visualize

Use this space to share your unfiltered feelings with zero judgment or criticism. Regardless of whether you feel your responses are negative or positive, write down your honest replies. Your answers are not "bad" either way—they simply exist to uncover what you need in order to embody your truest sense of self. You have to be willing to be radically honest to figure out the answers within your heart.

Imagine someone is describing you as a person. What words would they use to describe your personality? What roles would they say you hold?

_____

_____

_____

_____

_____

What aspects of your above response would you want to change? What aspects would you like to continue to hold as part of your identity?

_____

Imagine someone is explaining what you do for joy and fulfillment. What would they say you do in terms of hobbies, activities, work, and play? Would they say you are fulfilled with your life as it is now?

_____

_____

_____

_____

What aspects of your above response would you want to change? What aspects would you like to continue to hold as part of your identity?

_____

Imagine someone is describing you as a mother. What words would they use to describe you as a mom? Would they say you are fulfilled in your role as a mother?

_____

_____

_____

_____

_____

What aspects of your above response would you want to change? What aspects would you like to continue to hold as part of your identity?

_____

_____

Imagine someone is describing you as the very best version of yourself. They are raving about you as a wonderful and inspirational person and mother! How do they describe your personality, roles, hobbies, and modes of fulfillment? What would they say you do on a daily basis? How is it so clear to them that you are living a life of authenticity, alignment, and contentment?

_____

_____

_____

_____

_____

_____

_____

_____

_____

Let's Grow

Let's consider your core values, the identity traits you wish to embody, and the way you would like to show up in the world. Jot down a list of outlets that come to mind when you think about identity fulfillment. This can be a hobby, a creative project, a habit, or something that you feel called to try out.

_____   _____   _____

_____   _____   _____

_____   _____   _____

_____   _____   _____

_____   _____   _____

Now choose one form of fulfillment to focus on prioritizing this coming month. Circle it in your list above. Over the course of the month, color in one of the hearts below on each day that you take time to prioritize your chosen identity project. At the end of the month, answer the final reflection questions.

How did you feel when you prioritized this specific activity?

_____

_____

_____

_____

_____

_____

What is your plan for fulfillment going forward?

_____

_____

_____

_____

_____

What is another fulfillment opportunity that you would like to prioritize in the near future?

_____

_____

_____

_____

_____

| 8 |

Social Life

The Importance of Maintaining Social Time as a Parent

Life changes in so many ways once we become mothers, and, naturally, our social life is one area that begins to shift profoundly in terms of priorities, preferences, and possibilities.

Starting a family can often lead to a change in terms of what we want to do socially as well as what is feasible within our new role. In the same way that a career shift would change your weekly hours and paid time off, motherhood also has a huge impact on how you take time off to connect with others.

Although these changes can be viewed as a form of personal growth, and some of the shifts are welcomed with open arms—for example, I gladly traded heading out for a night on the town while it was snowing in midwinter for snuggling my baby on the couch instead—there are still many aspects of our social lives that should be prioritized even in motherhood.

"Daring to set boundaries is about having the courage to love ourselves, even when we risk disappointing others."

—BRENÉ BROWN

It's vital to understand what aspects of your social life you would like to continue to honor versus which items you would rather leave in the past. When you feel clear on what social experiences are actually fulfilling to you, you allow yourself to uncover meaningful experiences and connections that will bring value to your life.

When I was pregnant with my first daughter, I often heard the refrain "Do it now while you can." This phrase, which is often repeated to pregnant women ad nauseam (as if we weren't nauseated enough), is nerve-wracking! I recall thinking, "Will my social life really end when I have my baby?" I've always been an extroverted social butterfly, so it was scary to try to wrap my head around this idea while I was beginning not only my role as a mother but also my role as a stay-at-home mom. The answer to the question "Will my social life end" was of course no, but that doesn't

mean things wouldn't change. Life as a mother often requires more advanced planning, frequent compromises, and opting for child-friendly social outings with friends when possible. Our social lives as mothers do look different in many ways, but I'm here to tell you that you can still have a fulfilling social calendar once you become a mom—it'll just take a little reflection and planning.

Not even four months after my first daughter was born, the world shut down because of the COVID-19 pandemic, so my social interactions halted entirely. During lockdown, I spent a lot of time solo with my daughter while my husband was at work. I wanted to be a stay-at-home mom, but I hadn't intended to be stuck at home quite so much. The silver lining of this experience is that it forced me to genuinely consider what I missed about my social life. I began to learn, as the world opened back up, that not all social activities are created equal. Some

You can still have a fulfilling social calendar once you become a mom—it'll just take a little reflection and planning.

Be decisive about what you need.

things made me genuinely excited, whereas other things left me feeling overscheduled and dreading whatever event I had said yes to once the day arrived. I had to re-create boundaries and navigate obligatory invitations to find balance within my resurging social life.

When we think about meeting our social needs, it's important to remember that not all social activities are cup filling. It's extremely easy to forget or ignore this fact by saying yes to every single social invite that crosses your path. This can be especially true if you don't live close to friends or family, and so spontaneous or frequent social invites are rare, pushing you to feel obligated to accept everything offered. But you have to dig deep to recognize what types of social settings and groups fill you up so that you can capitalize on your limited time and energy. Be decisive about what you need. If a Sunday brunch is your cup of tea,

then prioritize that over an invitation to a Sunday afternoon child's birthday party. When you set these boundaries, some people may struggle with your choices, but ultimately everyone's life is busy, and if you consistently prioritize other people's feelings over your own, then you're going to find your cup overflowing with resentment. Naturally, we will all have some obligations or genuinely want to show up in a way that prioritizes other people over ourselves sometimes, but don't be afraid to prioritize what *you* want sometimes too. You're still a good person, even though you put yourself first!

There have been countless times when I have made plans and had to decline another set of plans because there simply isn't time to attend both events. By saying yes to one thing, we inadvertently say no to something else. You may know this by the term "opportunity cost": taking one

When you genuinely give yourself time to think about what you say yes or no to, you'll start making choices from a more meaningful place.

opportunity comes at the cost of losing the option to pursue a different opportunity. Of course, it's not a perfect math equation, but even if two events don't literally coincide, you still are running on limited energy and time. You can't do it all!

On the flip side, saying no means saying no: when you decline something, you leave the door open for something else—but you also close the door on what you declined. There's an important distinction to be made here between declining something and putting off the decision until later, and finding a balance between these two in your life is critical to meeting your social needs. When you're excited about something, say yes! When something is totally uninteresting to you, say no. When you're hesitant about something, then do just that: hesitate.

Think of a time when you immediately said yes to something, only to realize, as the activity approached, that you didn't want to attend. We've all been there. Sometimes it feels like you'd be willing to pay actual, cold, hard cash to be able to skip it and curl up on the couch instead. To avoid this scenario, it's beneficial to practice "the pause." This is pretty much exactly what it sounds like: it just means pausing before committing to anything. As an extroverted, recovering people pleaser with a general lack of boundaries, I used to find myself overcommitting nonstop. I love people! I crave time with others. I find joy in connecting and socializing, until I do not. This is why I find it very important to literally pause before agreeing to anything. This doesn't mean I say no! It just means I delay my answer so I can make a solid choice that works for me. Your natural instincts are often right, so trust them. If you are immediately overwhelmed by potentially saying yes (or no) to an activity, then pause and reconsider it later in the day.

Is your social calendar going to fill up as easily as it did prior to becoming a mother? Unlikely. There's no award for having a packed calendar, though, and, as moms, the quality-over-quantity rule really needs to take the driver's seat. Should you turn down every event just in case something better comes along? Or because your first instinct is "How will I fit this into my jam-packed schedule?" Heck, no! We would probably never do anything if we took that approach. But you can practice the pause when social invitations arise, to allow reflection on how they might or might not fit into your life. Time is a commodity, and you shouldn't be shelling it out willy-nilly. When you genuinely give yourself time to think about what you say yes or no to, you'll start making choices from a more meaningful place. Learning to prioritize

your social needs can be difficult in a world of obligations and expectations, but, at the end of the day, you simply cannot do it all, which is why I have found practicing the pause to be entirely life changing.

If you have trouble resisting the urge to give a clear yes or no in the moment, then have a go-to phrase in your pocket to allow yourself to delay your response gracefully. You could say something like "That sounds fun! I have to check my calendar, and I will get back to you," or "I can't commit right now, but once I plan out the week, I'll have a better idea of if I can do this or not." If needed, get clarity from the person inviting you as to a timeline for an RSVP or if one is required at all. Just don't forget to actually get back to the person in the end. If you fail to ever commit to anything socially, then unfortunately people may stop extending invitations to you. And do your best not to leave the door open on an invite in a way that makes people assume you're coming when you have

Be wary of falling into the trap of protecting your peace at all costs.

no real intention of doing so. This can create unnecessary drama or make people stop taking you at your word.

As a busy mom, there will be plenty of times when you have to say no to an invite, and, as we've seen, that's totally fine, and it usually means you're prioritizing the kinds of social events that will truly fill your cup. But be wary of falling into the trap of protecting your peace at all costs. It's easy to find yourself hunkering down and doing nothing now that you have children. Let's face it, it can be hard to gather up the kids, supplies, yourself, your partner, and everything else to make it to an event. Sometimes you have to divide and conquer, and it can be hard to attend an event solo so your partner can take over the childcare. Even harder sometimes can be finding a babysitter (and paying for one)! But if you constantly take the "easy

way out," decline everything, and tell yourself that you just don't have the time or energy to deal with a social life, over time you will end up dissatisfied, resentful, and craving adult connection because you aren't meeting one of your essential needs.

Sometimes we have to learn to sneak social interaction into our lives in unique ways, especially when we're juggling children, work, family, chores, and all of the many things we have on our plates. Maybe chatting on the phone with a friend once a week can take the place of getting together at a restaurant. A girls' weekend getaway sounds amazing, right? But is it feasible? Maybe not quite at the moment . . . so why not scale it back to a girls' staycation day date? Plan fun activities to do together for the entire day—maybe with the kids around, maybe without. When it's difficult to find childcare, social playdates with your girlfriends can be a lifesaver; you get to hang out while your kids play together. I've found this kind of social activity to be hugely beneficial for me, especially with my girls at their current ages. Since they're still not full-time school-aged, we are home together every day, so we all appreciate the break in routine and the socialization. Hangouts like these don't have to cost money—local libraries often have programs and story times, or check out one of your local parks for a fun afternoon outside. Alternating houses is another great way to have a fun, free play date where you don't have to focus on escape-artist toddlers or the public surrounding you.

In the previous chapters of this book, we've already touched upon several ways in which you can socialize in the context of fulfilling your other needs. We discussed, for example, getting together with friends for a workout session, or joining a club or community that inspires you. I've found that I genuinely appreciate a brunch or dinner with my girlfriends, a book club meeting, or events at my yoga studio more than the classic nighttime hangs of the previous stage of my life. I love the time to connect without the regret of exhaustion the following day. I crave these meaningful conversations with the people I love, and, after it's been too long, I start to notice that I'm antsy to see my friends again.

I know it's not easy to find the time. It takes genuine effort to get your schedule to match up with others', especially as more of your friends also begin having children. My tip is to set a date and stick to it if more than half of the invited people can still attend. Schedules will change, new obligations will pop up, someone or their kids will get sick, work will get in the way, and childcare will fall through. If your group cancels entirely each time something pops up, then getting together will quickly shift from once a month to once a year. Human beings are social creatures, so once-a-year get-togethers are not gonna fly! Extend the same grace to others as you like to have extended to you, show up when you can, and make sure you keep your social life alive as an integral part of a balanced lifestyle.

Let's Reflect

For this this-or-that style activity, you'll need a pencil as well as a marker or pen, preferably of a different color (not black). First, examine each set of items and use the pencil to circle which of the two you typically do. Then, switch to your marker, examine each set, and circle which of the two you prefer to do. If you are stuck between the two, consider which item you are craving most in the upcoming month. If you feel strongly that you need to incorporate both items into your life more often, then circle both! By the end, you'll be able to see two things at a glance: any disconnects between your preferences and your reality, and a guiding list of activities you should focus on doing more often.

One-on-one time
with a friend
or
seeing friends in a
group setting

Going to a quiet
dinner
or
attending an
exhilarating
concert

Heading to a
playdate at the
zoo
or
hosting a playdate
at home

Calling a friend on the
phone to catch up
or
chitchatting via text

Casual, low-key
plans
or
fancy, detailed
plans

Brunch with your
girlfriends
or
grabbing coffee
with a new friend

A weekend away
with kids
or
a weekend away
without kids

Socializing as a
family unit
or
socializing solo

Committing right
away or pausing
before saying yes
or
saying no

An evening out with
your significant
other

or

an evening in with
your significant
other

Going for a walk
with friends

or

going to see a movie
with friends

"No thank you" to a
child-centric event

or

"no thank you" to a
child-free event

Being a pro at
boundary setting

or

still learning how to
set boundaries

Planning recurring
social events

or

having spontaneous
plans

List here any social activities or categories that weren't included that are meaningful
to you.

_____

_____

_____

_____

_____

_____

_____

Let's Visualize

Consider what types of social interaction fill your cup. In a perfect world, what would your social life look like over the course of the next month? Try not to get too hung up on the details right now; just consider what social activities you are interested in adding to your life.

Think about your relationship with the words "yes" and "no." How do you currently set boundaries, or how do you wish to start setting better boundaries?

_____

_____

_____

_____

Think about "the pause" we discussed in this chapter. Write a go-to response sentence to help you practice the pause when an invitation arises that you aren't sure about.

_____

_____

_____

_____

What social activities leave you feeling rejuvenated versus depleted?

_____

_____

_____

_____

How would you prefer to connect with your family?

_____

_____

_____

_____

How would you prefer to connect with your partner or spouse?

_____

_____

_____

_____

_____

How would you prefer to connect with your friends?

_____

_____

_____

_____

What are some ways you can sneak social time in when childcare isn't available?

_____

_____

_____

_____

Let's Grow

Brainstorm in the boxes provided to lay out your favorite social activities.

Type of social activity	My ideas and favorites
Activities with kids	
Activities without kids	
Activities that recharge	
Activities that excite	
Activities with partner	
Activities with friends	

For the coming month, refer to the "wish list" you created on the facing page to try to complete one of each type of social activity listed in the chart below. Once you have completed each category, log your feelings about your experience.

Type of social activity	What did you do? With whom? Where?	How did you feel after doing this activity?
Activity with kids		
Activity without kids		
Activity that recharges		
Activity that excites		
Activity with partner		
Activity with friends		

Which activity did you enjoy most this month? How did it feel to set aside the time for this activity? Which social experience(s) would you like to make into regular habits?

_____

_____

|9|

It Takes a Village

Tapping Into the Support You Have and
Releasing Expectations of How It "Should Be"

We hear it so often as mothers: parenting takes a village. We
know this is true, but sometimes finding that village or accepting
its help is easier said than done. At times, we may even overlook
the support we have simply because we're wishing we had
people in our lives who could show up in a different way than
what is already being offered.

When searching for support people and support systems, it can
be easy to fall into the trap of comparison, where we see other
people's villages and wish they were our own. But when you take
the time to reflect on your specific needs and opportunities, you
might be surprised at the support you find all around you.

So, as we dive into this final chapter, it's important to first
acknowledge that everyone's situation is different. Support comes
in all shapes and sizes. Some moms may have a huge support
system consisting of a partner, family, and friends within walking
or driving distance, whereas others may feel entirely alone after a
big move or familial estrangements or losses.

*"We're here for a reason. I believe a bit of
that reason is to throw little torches out to
lead people through the dark."*

—WHOOPI GOLDBERG

We also have to understand that these varying levels and kinds of support don't diminish our value as parents. You are not less because you have access to and accept more support, and you are not flawed because you don't have support around you or you decline help from others. Your journey is yours and no one else's. Yes, at times we may feel a bit envious of the free babysitters so-and-so down the street has on call, but someone else could be simultaneously envious of the fact that *you* don't have to deal with daily unannounced pop-ins from the whole family! The grass is always greener, etc.

If there is a way to change your level of support to better fit your family's needs, then do it! What are you waiting for? The "easiest" and most obvious way to get help is by paying for it—hiring a babysitter so you can get work done around the house or opting for a regular housecleaner, for example. Ask yourself honestly if you have the budget for these kinds of help, and figure out if they're right for your family logistically and financially. Beyond paying for the help you need, though, you may be ignoring a gold mine of support in the family and friends who surround you. I find people often offer their support with the phrase "Let me know what I can do to help." What if you actually tapped into that resource? I have heard of friends and neighbors sharing school pick-up duties to

better work around naptimes, parents taking advantage of the free childcare playrooms at rec centers to sneak in a workout, and schoolmates having alternating playdates at one another's homes so parents can head to doctor's appointments or run errands. If you have a supportive family nearby, this could look like accepting the offer of an aunt, uncle, or grandparent to take the kids to a movie or the park for an afternoon.

One thing that can work well is tossing out an open-ended request for help, such as "Hey, if you have any free time next week to watch the kids, let me know." This puts the ball in the other person's court in times when you don't have a specific scheduled or pressing need. Sometimes, no one will be available, and you can either modify plans to make something work or bring the child(ren) along with you for an errand or appointment. Ultimately, I choose to still do many things even when it means adding the extra time and energy required to do them with my three little helpers. Luckily for me, I actually do my best grocery shopping with my children, because I can verbally narrate everything we need to the kids. In moments like these, my kids are a mini support system! I promise you, when I go to the grocery store alone, I am way more likely to forget something versus when I go with any or all of my kids.

The concept of leaning into support comes more naturally to some than

You are not less of a mom because you accept help.

others. At the start of my mothering journey, I often found it difficult to accept when someone offered help. This seems like a champagne problem, doesn't it? Who wouldn't want an extra pair of hands? However, the more moms I spoke to, the more I realized that this problem wasn't unique to me. In hindsight, it really does seem silly that I turned down so many offers of support, but it was anything but silly to me and those other moms in the moment.

As a brand-new mom trying to figure out your new lifelong role and working to form a relationship with your new baby, your brain might struggle to comprehend that people are offering to help simply to be helpful. Your mind may twist things up and make you feel that accepting help from others means that you are in some way inferior. You might believe that if you say yes to help, it means people will think you can't do it on your own. Although it took me some time to reach this conclusion, I finally realized that, sure, we may be capable of pushing through and doing every single thing on our own, but to what end? Is it worth it to be left feeling depleted simply to say you were a "strong, independent woman"? We have all heard "It takes a village" time and time again, so if you have a village, or even just one person stepping up with a helping hand, tap into that resource shamelessly. You are not less of a mom because you accept help.

Growing up, I remember my Grammy would regularly pop in on her way to the grocery store to see if my mom needed anything. It was entirely normal for my mom to say, "Yeah, we could use a loaf of bread" or "Can you grab a gallon of milk?" At the time, I had no clue how helpful this really was, but now, as a mom of three, I realize that when someone else can grab an item or two from the store for me, it truly lessens the load.

My husband will often stop at the grocery store to grab a few odds and ends on his way home from work. I know this scenario has a little bit of a

bad reputation in the modern world. I've seen many a video out there joking about how husbands take the time to go to the store and just get home even later than normal when the mom is in need of helping hands sooner, or how the husband is incapable of bringing home the correct groceries in the first place. Cue the mom ripping her hair out! Cue the resentment! These jokes are all well and good—as long as you understand that they are stereotypes, and as long as you maintain good and clear communication with your partner so that they don't become the joke.

In truth, "joke" scenarios like these can serve as good learning examples for you to parse what support should look like for you personally. Support might

If there is an imbalance in the mental load in a parenting partnership, then a conversation needs to happen as soon as possible.

mean your partner goes to the store for you, or it might mean you going to the store alone to grab the items yourself while your partner takes over the childcare. Personally, I love that my husband walks in the door with the groceries. I also thoroughly appreciate that he takes responsibility for knowing what those groceries need to be before I tell him! In any case, you are not "picky" or "needy" when you express specific support needs or request that others show up for you in a slightly different way than they have been doing.

This brings us to one huge underlying type of support that's gained a lot of attention in our culture lately, and rightfully so: the mental load. The mental load is all the background things we have to think about and plan for in order to keep our family unit running smoothly. There's a lot in there! Like me, you probably spend a huge chunk of your time planning activities, meals, appointments, parties, and more. But the mental load also includes things like keeping an eye on grades, laundry, email, how your kid likes their hair done in the morning, who needs what medicines at what times of day . . . so many things big and small, but boy, do they add up.

It's very important to have a conversation—indeed, regular conversations—about mental load with your spouse or partner. If you don't, you may feel a lack of support without quite realizing where it's coming from, which can quickly lead to a dark vortex of repressed emotions. Let's take party planning as an example. There are some things I think about when planning a kid's party that wouldn't even register in my husband's mind. A homemade balloon arch for our daughter's first birthday? He would deem this entirely unnecessary. Honestly, a balloon *anything* would never even blip on his radar. The decor is something that's important to me and not to him. I support him by taking control of that area, and he supports me by being the one to order all the food and stock the fridge with drinks. We tap into our different skill sets and balance each other. We are a team. Importantly, we both recognize that the other person is taking on a separate mental load of their own when it comes to planning the party.

If there is an imbalance in the mental load in a parenting partnership, then a conversation needs to happen as soon as possible. There have been times when my husband and I have each thought we were supporting the other, only to realize that each of us felt lopsided in the division of duties. This meant no one felt supported. What happens when no one feels supported? Anger, resentment, frustration, and burnout—nothing good!

What should be evident by now is that support is not just about who can watch your kids so you can be left alone to get things done. It is just as much, if not more, about what happens

Show your littlest family members how to support you. Provide them with the opportunity to learn how to show empathy, teamwork, and pride in their role within the family unit.

within the walls of your home, because this is where you spend so much of your life. A babysitter for four hours isn't going to cure the burnout you feel in the remaining twenty hours of the day. You need to focus on small, sustainable changes that make you feel supported over time.

Let's talk more about how to get your support needs met inside the home. I've heard testimonies from many mothers who felt burnt out, unfulfilled, and left with no time to cherish themselves because the mental and physical loads were not balanced in their family. This includes the division of household labor, which isn't just a question of which partner does what—it's also about the kids. I've begun to involve my

children in balancing the load as they have gotten older. As I mentioned in a previous chapter, my two- and four-year-olds bring their plates to the sink after mealtimes and wipe their hands and faces. Did this happen overnight? Absolutely not. But now that it does happen without nagging (most of the time—come on, they're not robots), it really makes me feel supported. The simple act of every person clearing their plate after a meal is not just truly helpful in the cleanup process—it also teaches the kids that I'm not their maid and that they are just as responsible for their personal cleanup as I am for mine. Many hands make less work. Have we had spills while they learn to balance and walk with their plates? Oh, yes, we have. But guess what—that's a great opportunity to teach them how to clean up a spill!

I know people who have included their children in tasks such as this from an early age, and they've all expressed how, down the line, as the kids grew older, the kids were willing and ready to step up and take ownership of doing their part for the family. I don't know about you, but I'm willing to try it out now (and break a few plates) so that in ten years I'm not alone in the kitchen cleaning up all the plates myself and lamenting that "no one ever helps" and "I always have to do everything." The thought alone makes me feel sad—no thanks! Show your littlest family

members how to support you. Provide them with the opportunity to learn how to show empathy, teamwork, and pride in their role within the family unit. This is their home too—so don't write them off.

At the end of the day, the levels of support that each individual mother has vary deeply. The needs that each mother has also change throughout the different seasons of motherhood and life in general. There is no simple formula when it comes to support needs, so it's vital to uncover your unique needs and opportunities when attempting to create your village.

Let's Reflect

It's time to sit down and take stock of what your current support system looks like. For this activity, check always, sometimes, or never for each prompt. Then read the journaling questions on the facing page, consider your responses to the prompts, and use them to guide your answers.

ALWAYS	SOMETIMES	NEVER	
○	○	○	I have support from family members.
○	○	○	I feel supported in regard to the mental load.
○	○	○	My support system is strong.
○	○	○	I find it easy to ask for help when I need it.
○	○	○	I have support from my partner or spouse.
○	○	○	My partner and I are mutually supportive.
○	○	○	My children play a role in family support.
○	○	○	I have access to childcare on weekends.
○	○	○	I have access to childcare on weekdays.
○	○	○	I feel supported in terms of household duties.
○	○	○	I take steps to show self-support.
○	○	○	I have support from friends, neighbors, or coworkers.
○	○	○	My general opinion of my current "village" is positive.
○	○	○	I can rely on my support people.

In which area do I always feel supported? How/why?

_____

_____

In which area do I sometimes feel supported? How/why?

_____

_____

In which area do I never feel supported? How/why not?

_____

_____

Which area is your number one priority to address going forward?

_____

_____

Which area is your number two priority to address going forward?

_____

_____

Which area is your number three priority to address going forward?

_____

_____

Let's Visualize

As you begin to visualize what your levels of support should look like going forward, it's important to remember that you can't wave a magic wand to conjure support that doesn't exist. At times, we have to get creative with the support we have. As you answer the following questions, try to be realistic—visualization as a tool is most effective when it's realistic.

On the lines below, jot down any areas or tasks that you could use support with right now. Try to be specific (e.g., rather than just writing "housework," write "putting away the laundry").

_____ _____ _____

_____ _____ _____

_____ _____ _____

_____ _____ _____

_____ _____ _____

Now look at your above list. Which of these items can you immediately ask for help with from a partner, friend, or family member?

Task: _____   Who can help: _____

Task: _____   Who can help: _____

Task: _____   Who can help: _____

Task: _____   Who can help: _____

Task: _____   Who can help: _____

Task: _____   Who can help: _____

In the chart below, consider what your support currently looks like, then consider what changes you would like to realistically see in each category. If a change is not currently possible, how can you find peace with your circumstances through gratitude instead?

	Current status of support (or lack thereof)	Support goals (or how you can make peace with the status quo)
From my spouse or partner		
Within my household		
From my extended family		
From my friends		
In regard to the mental load		
Other support (such as paid services)		

Let's Grow

Since moms are constantly inundated with the message that we can "do it all," asking for help or support can be much easier said than done. Now that you have worked hard to uncover your individual support needs and the areas where you require more support, you must take the next step.

In the space provided, write a letter to someone you trust, detailing the main areas that would make you feel supported and lighten your load. This letter could be to your spouse or partner, a specific family member, a close friend, or even your children.

Be sure to include tangible tasks that you could use help with, as well as tasks related to the mental load of parenting. What support are you currently craving from this person? In what ways does this person already show you support? Express gratitude for that. How can you build upon the current level of support to better fit your lifestyle and family in your present phase of life? Be sure also to explain the ways you have already been advocating for your needs. How could this person help you on that ongoing path of self-care?

When you are finished writing, consider sharing this letter with the person directly or having a conversation with the person to see how you can work together to achieve these goals.

It's vital to uncover your unique needs and opportunities when attempting to create your village.

Dear _____

_____

_____

_____

_____

_____

_____

_____

_____

_____

_____

_____

_____

_____

_____

_____

_____

_____

Putting It All Together

Wow, you made it! At this point, you have been reading, reflecting, visualizing, and growing for nine months. This is nothing short of an amazing accomplishment. I'm so proud of you! I hope you're also proud of yourself. On our journey together, we have considered everything from basic survival and physical needs to deeper mental and emotional needs related to identity and self-fulfillment. What a trip! Now it's time to tie everything together and decide where you will go from here.

Answer the following questions to solidify your future by visualizing your goals and recognizing your growth over the course of our time together throughout the past several months. Your responses should focus on what you plan to achieve, combined with what you have already achieved. Use positive words and phrases to propel yourself forward in the direction you want to go, rather than dwelling on the things holding you back.

Consider the single motivational word you selected at the beginning of this book as you answer this final set of questions Write your word below to guide you.

My Word:

_____

How do you feel on a daily basis? What does an average day look like for you?

_____
_____
_____
_____
_____
_____

How will you nourish your body through food?

_____
_____
_____
_____
_____
_____

What is your nightly routine and how do you prioritize adequate rest?

_____
_____
_____
_____
_____
_____

In what ways do you take pride in your presentation of self?

_____

_____

_____

_____

_____

_____

What does quiet time look like for you?

_____

_____

_____

_____

_____

_____

How do you incorporate intentional movement into your life?

_____

_____

_____

_____

_____

_____

What hobbies or activities make you feel fulfilled and content?

_____

_____

_____

_____

_____

_____

What do you like to do with your family, friends, spouse, etc.?

_____

_____

_____

_____

_____

How do you feel supported by others? How do you support yourself?

_____

_____

_____

_____

_____

Now, for one bonus month as you work to tie everything together, use the symbols and calendar provided to track each time you meet one of the following needs. At the end of the month, compare your results to the calendar that you filled out in the very first chapter, back when we embarked on this journey together. Revel in the changes you have made over these last months!

Basic Physical Needs	Personal and Mental Needs	Social Needs	Support Needs
✓	♡	☺	☆

1   2   3   4   5   6

7   8   9   10   11   12

13   14   15   16   17   18

19   20   21   22   23   24

25   26   27   28   29   30

Thank You

Thank you from the bottom of my heart for joining me within the pages of this book. I hope that you have taken adequate time to reflect, visualize, and grow. Remember that this journey to embodiment is a lifelong trek. You'll still have hard moments or days, but now, with self-love in mind, you'll be better equipped to respond to and recover from the ups and downs that life and motherhood bring. Please be sure to come back to this journal not only in difficult times but also in joyful times. Remember to be proud of your progress, and do not forget to celebrate your immense growth. Whenever you feel a little lost, always return to this unwavering truth: You are worthy of the beautiful life you envision!

About the Author

Abigail Dosen is a passionate book blogger, writer, stylist, and mother. A former English teacher, Abigail graduated from The Ohio State University with a bachelor's degree in middle-childhood education with endorsements in English, reading, social studies, and science. She is the founder of @adosenbooks, a vibrant social media book community and book club for mothers, where she shares her love for literature and supports fellow moms on their journeys.

Index

A

appearance. *See* personal appearance

B

Bookstagram, 100–101, 112–13
brain, "cleansing," 66–67

C

COVID-19 shutdown, 25, 124–25

E

eating and mealtime. *See* nourishment
exercise (let's get moving), 93–107
    about: overview of benefits and challenges, 93–94
    accountability partner, 99, 101
    active recovery, 94–95
    balanced approach, 94–95
    Bookstagram monthly challenge, 100–101
    cycle-syncing, 95–97
    family workouts, 99
    free, local options, 101
    group class or in-gym workout, 101
    guidelines for, 94–101
    Let's Grow, 106–7
    Let's Reflect, 102
    Let's Visualize, 103–5
    motivation and commitment, 97, 99–101
    working into schedule, 97–99

F

fulfillment. *See* personal fulfillment
future, visualizing. *See* Let's Visualize

G

growth mindset, 14
guilt. *See* mom guilt

I

"If You Leave a Paper Towel on the Counter: A Memoir," 39

J

journal, guided. *See also* Let's Grow; Let's Reflect; Let's Visualize
    about: this book as, 8–9
    chapter structure overview, 15
    guide to using, 14
    kickoff activities, 16–21
    putting it all together, 150–53
journal time, 82

L

let's get moving. *See* exercise (let's get moving)
Let's Grow
    about: initial exercise (choosing one word as your guide), 20–21; overview of, 15
    exercise (let's get moving), 106–7
    mindful rest, 58–59
    nourishment and mealtime, 46–47
    personal appearance, 72–73
    personal fulfillment, 120–21
    quiet time, 90–91
    self-love and self-care, 34–35
    social life, 134–35
    support (it takes a village), 148–49
Let's Reflect
    about: initial exercise (identifying words that resonate with you), 16–17; overview of, 15
    exercise (let's get moving), 102
    mindful rest, 54–55
    nourishment and mealtime, 42–43
    personal appearance, 68–69
    personal fulfillment, 116–17
    quiet time, 86–87
    self-love and self-care, 30–31
    social life, 130–31
    support (it takes a village), 144–45
Let's Visualize
    about: initial exercise (five words aligning with your vision of life), 18–19; overview of, 15
    exercise (let's get moving), 103–5
    mindful rest, 56–57
    nourishment and mealtime, 44–45
    personal appearance, 70–71
    personal fulfillment, 118–19
    quiet time, 88–89
    self-love and self-care, 32–33
    social life, 132–33
    support (it takes a village), 146–47
levels of needs. *See* needs, levels of

M

mealtime. *See* nourishment
mental load, support and, 141–42
mindful rest, 49–59
    about: overview of, 49
    daily quiet time and, 84–85 (*See also* quiet time)
    importance of, 50
    intentional use of quiet time before bed, 51–53
    Let's Grow, 58–59
    Let's Reflect, 54–55
    Let's Visualize, 56–57
    prioritizing with intentional habits, 49–53
    steps to establish routine of, 50–51
mom guilt, 24–27, 42, 78, 81

N

needs, levels of, 27–29
    about: mom guilt and, 25
    Level 1: basic physical needs, 28, 32 (*See also* exercise (let's get moving); mindful rest; nourishment; personal appearance)
    Level 2: personal and mental needs, 28, 32 (*See also* personal fulfillment; quiet time; self-love and self-care)
    Level 3: social needs, 29, 33 (*See also* social life)
    Level 4: support needs, 29, 33 (*See also* support (it takes a village))
    putting it all together, 150–53
nourishment, 37–48
    benefits of paying attention to your food, 40
    embracing meals as source of fuel and loving kindness, 37–42
    "If You Leave a Paper Towel on the Counter: A Memoir," 39
    Let's Grow, 46–47
    Let's Reflect, 42–43
    Let's Visualize, 44–45
    setting the example, 40–41
    sitting still lesson and, 38–41

P

personal and mental needs, 28, 32. *See also* personal fulfillment; quiet time; self-love and self-care

personal appearance, 61–73
about: overview of, 61
"cleansing" your brain and, 66–67
daily reality and, 62–63
embracing with pride, 61–67
hygiene and, 61, 62
Let's Grow, 72–73
Let's Reflect, 68–69
Let's Visualize, 70–71
nails and, 63–65
pampering yourself, 62
points to consider, 63
prioritizing rituals for, 65

personal fulfillment, 109–21
about: overview of, 109
author's story, 110, 111–13
creative outlet for, 112–13
Let's Grow, 120–21
Let's Reflect, 116–17
Let's Visualize, 118–19
motherhood, personal identity and, 114–15
personal nature of, 110–11
responsibility for, 110–11
self-value and, 113
work/jobs and, 113–15

physical needs (basic), 28, 32. *See also* exercise (let's get moving); mindful rest; nourishment; personal appearance
putting it all together, 150–53

Q

quiet time, 75–91. *See also* mindful rest
about: overview of, 75
after-the-kids-go-to-bed for, 80–81
early-morning wake-up for, 80
frustration, anger, poor-me and, 79
importance of, 76–78
journal time and, 82
with kids present, 78–79, 81, 82, 83
Let's Grow, 90–91
Let's Reflect, 86–87
Let's Visualize, 88–89

not all times are created equal, 79, 80, 84–85
outside the house (job, driving, etc.), 82–84
overstimulation/overwhelm and, 76–78, 84–85
realizations about, 79–80
screen time and, 81
while kids are awake, or napping, 81–82

quotes
Angelou, Maya, 61
Ball, Lucille, 23
Ban Breathnach, Sarah, 75
Brown, Brené, 123
Dyer, Wayne, 28
Goldberg, Whoopi, 137
Loren, Sophia, 109
Michaels, Jillian, 93
Radmacher, Mary Anne, 49
Wigmore, Ann, 37

R

rest. *See* mindful rest

S

sabotaging yourself. *See* mom guilt
screen time, quiet time and, 81
self-care for mothers. *See* self-love and self-care
self-discovery, using this book. *See also* Let's Grow; Let's Reflect; Let's Visualize
about: self-discovery and, 12–22
author's background and perspective, 8–9, 10–11
chapter structure overview, 15
self-love and self-care
about: overview of self-discovery and, 8–9; unpacking varying levels of self-care, 23–29
genuine needs and (*See* needs, levels of)
growth mindset for, 14
Let's Grow, 34–35
Let's Reflect, 30–31
Let's Visualize, 32–33
mom guilt and, 24–27, 42, 78, 81
patience/perseverance in quest for, 12–13
small daily choices, 14

time needed to learn about, 12
tree analogy, 24

social life, 123–35
about: importance of, 123; social needs and, 29, 33 (*See also* support (it takes a village))
author's story, 124–25
COVID-19 shutdown and, 124–25
declining invitations, 125–27, 128
delaying invitation responses, 127–28
Let's Grow, 134–35
Let's Reflect, 130–31
Let's Visualize, 132–33
prioritizing your needs, 125–27
sneaking it in to the schedule, 128–29
sticking to schedules, 129

support (it takes a village), 137–49
about: needs for, 29, 33; overview of, 137
asking for/finding more, 138
changing your level of, 138
getting needs met inside the home, 142–43
leaning into, 138–40
Let's Grow, 148–49
Let's Reflect, 144–45
Let's Visualize, 146–47
mental load and, 141–42
varying levels of availability, 138
your husband/partner and, 140–41

V

village, raising children and. *See* support (it takes a village)

W

words that stand out to you
identifying words that resonate with you, 16–17
narrowing down to your five top words, 20–21
selecting one word as your guide, 20–21

BETTER DAY BOOKS®

HAPPY · CREATIVE · CURATED

Business is personal at Better Day Books. We were founded on the belief that all people are creative and that making things by hand is inherently good for us. It's important to us that you know how much we appreciate your support. The book you are holding in your hands was crafted with the artistic passion of the author and brought to life by a team of wildly enthusiastic creatives who believed it could inspire you. If it did, please drop us a line and let us know about it. Connect with us on Instagram, post a photo of your art, and let us know what other creative pursuits you are interested in learning about. It all matters to us. You're kind of a big deal.

it's a good day to have a better day!®

www.betterdaybooks.com

better_day_books